AFRICAN SOCIETY TODAY

Farm labour

This book highlights the most important attributes of farm labour, how it is mobilized and controlled, and places it within a context of historical change.

International trade, colonialism, the growth of towns and transport have all exerted a powerful influence on rural Africa; yet agriculture is still dominated by small-commodity producers who have retained control over their means of production. More recently post-colonial states have attempted to reshape agriculture and transform rural societies. All these forces have altered traditional forms of agricultural production and distribution, but not sufficiently to undermine their labour-intensive character. Labour remains a crucial input into African farming and it often proves to be a major constraint on production. Many small farmers now produce for local or international markets and this shift towards greater commodity production has been achieved by new patterns of work and labour organization. Domestic production and family labour have been expanded or reduced by the spread of hired labour, as workers are redistributed between richer and poorer farmers and developed and underdeveloped regions. In addition, women have become more important as field labourers, as off-farm work for men becomes part of household reproduction.

AFRICAN SOCIETY TODAY

General editor: ROBIN COHEN

Advisory editors: O. Aribiah, Jean Copans, Paul Lubeck, Philip M. Mbithi, M. S. Muntemba, O. Nnoli, Richard Sandbrook

The series has been designed to provide scholarly, but lively and up-to-date, books, likely to appeal to a wide readership. The authors will be drawn from the field of development studies and all the social sciences, and will also have had experience of teaching and research in a number of African countries.

The books will deal with the various social groups and classes that comprise contemporary African society and successive volumes will link with previous volumes to create an integrated and comprehensive picture of the Africal social structure.

Also in the series

The politics of Africa's economic stagnation. RICHARD SANDBROOK
Migrant laborers. SHARON STICHTER

FARM LABOUR

KEN SWINDELL

Senior Lecturer, Department of Geography
and Associate of the Centre of West African Studies,
University of Birmingham

The right of the
University of Cambridge
to print and sell
all manner of books
was granted by
Henry VIII in 1534.
The University has printed
and published continuously
since 1584.

CAMBRIDGE UNIVERSITY PRESS

Cambridge
London New York New Rochelle
Melbourne Sydney

CAMBRIDGE UNIVERSITY PRESS
Cambridge, New York, Melbourne, Madrid, Cape Town,
Singapore, São Paulo, Delhi, Tokyo, Mexico City

Cambridge University Press
The Edinburgh Building, Cambridge CB2 8RU, UK

Published in the United States of America by Cambridge University Press, New York

www.cambridge.org
Information on this title: www.cambridge.org/9780521272124

First published 1985
Re-issued 2011

A catalogue record for this publication is available from the British Library

Library of Congress Catalogue Card Number: 85–5729

ISBN 978-0-521-25117-4 Hardback
ISBN 978-0-521-27212-4 Paperback

CONTENTS

FIGURES

TABLES

INTRODUCTION

The organization of farm labour in Africa has traditionally revolved around systems of kinship and descent, chieftaincy, public office and servitude. Unlike Europe and Latin America, access to labour, not land, was the basis of economic and political power in a continent where population densities were low and where land was frequently vested in communities rather than individuals. During the nineteenth century the development of export crops led to significant changes in farming, changes which were accentuated by the establishment of colonial rule, which in Central and Eastern Africa included the settlement of Europeans and the alienation of land. New crops created new demands for labour which were only partially satisfied from the internal resources of the commercial crop zones. Therefore labour was drawn from areas with little or no potential for the cultivation of export crops. By the 1930s reservoirs of migrant labour were well established throughout tropical Africa, and seasonal and circulatory migration have become associated with both commercial and food staple cultivation. The seasonality of farm work is a conspicuous 'feature' of African agriculture, as the alternation of wet and dry periods creates an uneven demand for labour, except in the few areas where irrigation is practised.

The supply of, and productivity of, farm labour in general depends on the potential stock, which is shaped by levels of fertility and mortality, health, the length of time individuals work, and the returns from farm work of different kinds, together with the relative returns from non-farm work if it is available. But in Africa, where the majority of farming is carried on by domestic groups, the size and composition of such groups and the principles of labour organization they use are of primary importance. Age, sex and kin have traditionally structured domestic labour – and they have by no means been abandoned; but over the past thirty years extended or complex groups have declined, and domestic production and reproduction have become more dependent on non-farm jobs, while there is increasing economic differentiation among peasant farmers. The commercialization of farming and increased levels of monetization in the rural economy have introduced new constraints on the supply of farm labour. These have been solved partly by changes in the sexual division of labour and in many places the role of women has been radically changed. In addition, hired labour has become much more pervasive and there are transfers of labour from poorer households to better-off small commodity producers. There now exists not only a seasonal and geographical redeployment of labour, but a social one as well.

The methods of hiring and paying farm labour are complex and it is difficult to assess wages. Workers may be paid in kind or as a fixed daily wage, and in the majority of cases farm work is seasonal and combined with some other forms of employment. Domestic groups may contain those who work on family farms, those who work for other farmers, or those who have permanent or seasonal jobs in the non-farm sector. On the one hand work outside the household limits its agricultural potential, but on the other it may be vital to its reproduction. Farm and non-farm labour are in many cases competitive and conjunctive categories. All this speaks of the imperfect specialization of labour between farm and factory, town and countryside, and stems from the fact that a majority of Africans still have rights to farmland. A landless or 'land-poor' labour force does exist, and corporate land tenure is declining, but these conditions are most apparent on the peripheries of large towns, in commercial farming areas, and in new agricultural schemes run by the State. The intervention of the State through programmes of agricultural reconstruction has added a new dimension to farming, but it has met with considerable resistance from peasants who have not been completely separated from their means of production and who act to preserve the interest of domestic groups rather than to serve the interest of the State. Conflict between private employers and employees outside the plantation sector, which is not included here, is often less obvious and takes the form of hard bargaining, trickery and cheating on both sides. The making of an agricultural wage labour force is in progress, but it is by no means complete.

Our knowledge of the mobilization, control and organization of farm labour comes from diverse sources and disciplines which have their own particular theoretical bases and methodologies. One important source is that of farm surveys which look at the economics of small-holder farming, usually in the context of complete farming seasons and cultivation cycles. The approach is in general behaviourist, emphasizing the role of African farmers as rational men operating small-scale farming units in a variety of market and non-market situations. This method of studying rural producers has become known as 'farming systems analysis': it is particularly interested in the allocation of resources, input–output relationships and the local constraints on farm production and productivity, such as land and labour (see, for example, Cleave, 1974; Collinson,

1972; Norman, 1972, 1980; Haswell, 1953, 1963; Levi and Havinden, 1982; Richards *et al.*, 1973; Richards, 1983).[1] African farming systems have much in common with household budget surveys and studies of entrepreneurship, although farming systems are much more concerned with cultivation techniques and ecological problems (see, for example, Hill, 1963, 1970, 1972; Berry, 1975; Hogendorn, 1978; Tiffen, 1976).

Critics of farm and village surveys point out that they are frequently small-scale, particularist and ahistorical, looking at villages as discrete entities and ignoring their external linkages. But these surveys of rural communities and households have raised some important issues and provided much empirical material, especially about the problems experienced by farmers over the seasonal supply of labour. However, while many studies are good at explaining the success or failure of individual farmers and production units within political and economic systems, the 'system' itself is frequently left out of the analysis (Apthorpe, 1977).

In contrast to farm surveys and farmers as decision makers, there is the 'structural-historical' approach of those working within a Marxist tradition, such as Meillasoux (1964, 1972, 1981); Suret-Canale (1964); Rey (1969, 1975); Terray (1972) and Godelier (1977). One important issue for Marxist writers (particularly in the 1970s) has been the identification of pre-capitalist formations through the modes of production which characterize them and their place within the materialist conception of history.[2] The transformation of pre-capitalist relations of production has

[1] A useful and comprehensive survey of research on agricultural development is provided by Eicher and Baker (1982).

[2] Introductions and surveys of pre-capitalist societies are provided by Crummey and Stewart (1981); Kahn and Llobera (1981); and Seddon (1978). For critiques of modes of production and pre-capitalist societies, see Brown (1984) and Law (1978).

led to an extended debate on peasantries and peasantization in Africa, the development of class-relations and the emergence of capitalist farmers and an agricultural proletariat. These debates have often proved contentious, but they have reinforced the historical perspective on rural communities as opposed to the frequent cross-sectional, ahistorical accounts of farm surveys. Furthermore, the discussion of pre-capitalist formations and their transformation has emphasized the social relations of production. Farming is certainly about tools, techniques and the control of nature, but the control of nature is also about the control of one set of people by another and their access to resources and benefits (Wallman, 1979).

Unfortunately, farm labour displays a complexity which is not easily described or fitted into neat categories. It is often easier to measure the hoe and the field than the internal and external production relationships into which farmers enter. This is because, although tools and techniques are varied, they are relatively direct in controlling nature and have undergone little modification over the centuries. But the social organization of production is more fluid, and, over the past one hundred years, in a period which encompasses European colonialism and African Independence, traditional systems of labour-use have been subjected to a wide spectrum of economic and political pressures. Furthermore, despite the introduction of mechanized farming, increases in population and the signs of land shortage, labour remains quantitatively and qualitatively dominant in the agricultural production process over most of tropical Africa.

A central theme of this book is how African farmers and farm labour have responded to changes brought about by diverse political and economic circumstances. Yet change has been patchy and has not occurred either simultaneously or with any kind of linearity over time and space. Although, for example, the penetration of European merchant capital and colonialism have had profound effects on African agriculture, they acted on non-capitalist systems which displayed substantial differences and on regions with widely differing pre-colonial histories. General structural changes were refracted through the prisms of African experience and history to produce localized patterns of change adaptation and resistance. Equally, the changes initiated by European intervention and colonial rule differed from one part of the continent to another. In West Africa imperialism was geared to the sale of crops grown by Africans and the purchase of European goods. In Central Africa in Zaire, Angola, Zimbabwe and Zambia, pre-colonial trading was disrupted and African farming was not encouraged; rather, Europeans were eager to recruit or force men into work in the mines and on plantations. Indigenous relations of production did not die in the late nineteenth century, and in many parts of Africa they have lingered on, but much of their former autonomy has been muted or eroded (see Crummey and Stewart, 1981; Birmingham and Martin, 1983).

This book cannot claim to offer any kind of comprehensive survey of farm labour in tropical Africa. Many parts of the continent receive little or no coverage, which is not a reflection of their unimportance but of on the one hand the author's interest in certain countries and on the other the limits imposed by a book of some 60,000 words. Some things have been deliberately left out, notably any discussion of plantations and plantation workers, because these will be dealt with in another book in this series. In the first chapter we look at the agricultural production process, especially patterns of work and the seasonal deployment of farm labour. After this outline of farming practice, Chapter 2 looks at how farm labour is organized within domestic groups, where the relations of production are structured by age, sex and kin. Chapters 3 and 4 consider how the traditional organization and use of farm labour have been affected by the market economy, and how it has altered the division of labour within farming households, as well as accelerating economic differentiation and the use of hired labour. Although hired labour is quite common now, there are other means of recruiting non-domestic labour through forms of communal labour which extend beyond the household or kin. Workgroups and systems of labour exchange are part of the history and development of African farming and Chapter 5 discusses their growth, decline and adaptation and speculates on their role in agrarian change. The final chapter dwells on an important contemporary issue, that of the peasant farmer and the State.

1

PATTERNS OF WORK: THE USE AND DEPLOYMENT OF FARM LABOUR

Agricultural technology is an expression of man's method of dealing with nature to secure a particularly important part of his needs and wants. But technology includes not just tools and cultivation systems, but how farm labour is used in the production process, who does what (the technical division of labour), how much labour and what type is used, and when it is required (the deployment of labour). The *when* can be of crucial importance in the tropics, where the alternation of wet and dry seasons is very marked and where seasonal workloads dominate agricultural activity. Even under technologically-advanced systems of farming, agricultural production is not entirely free of nature, which influences the rhythm of production and levels of output. Also, agricultural products have a shorter life than industrial ones, and perishability, depredation by pests and storage problems heighten the risks undertaken by agricultural producers. Compared with industry, agricultural production is spread over a longer time period and can be subject to bursts of intense activity, separated by periods of rest. Therefore when we discuss the use and distribution of labour, it is not only by age, sex, and hours worked, but by its distribution throughout the farming year.

It will become apparent that this chapter is primarily descriptive and concerned with patterns of work; it is also about how farmers cope with physical externalities embedded within particular cultivation systems, which make specific demands on the stock and flow of labour. There are two reasons for beginning with these issues: first, because they are a prelude to and an integral part of our subsequent concern with the social relationships into which farmers enter as part of the production process; second, because they should form part of planned programmes of agrarian change. Planners have frequently set to work with a limited understanding of farming techniques and how labour is used, which in part explains the resistance by peasants to the introduction of agro-technology. Yet those who have spent any time with farmers, and have bothered to ask them about their work, have usually found them to be articulate and well aware of the nature and extent of their farming problems. Even when farmers are not fully aware of the external forces which create many of their difficulties they are nonetheless faced with the immediacy of them, and the necessity for practical solutions. The 'art of the possible' is not only the catch-phrase of the politician, but also part of the African farmer's vocabulary, especially the small-scale domestic producer who lacks the safety-net of subsidies available to capitalist farmers in developed countries.

CULTIVATION SYSTEMS

One way of distinguishing different cultivation systems in Africa is to look at the frequency of cropping. At one end of the scale there is food gathering, and at the other multiple cropping, where two or more crops are produced from the same piece of land with no fallow period. In between these extensive and intensive forms of production lie systems with varying periods of fallow. Boserup (1965) has classified these as forest-fallows, bush-fallows and short-fallows. Also, there are annual cultivation systems where farming is restricted to the wet season, with a very short fallow during the dry season when the land is left idle. The frequency of cultivation is related to the method of restoring soil fertility; under forest-fallows the regeneration of woody species and grasses replaces lost humus and nutrients, whereas under short-fallows and annual cultivation there has to be an increased use of animal dung, artificial fertilizers, human waste or compound sweepings. Floodland cultivation – both seasonal and continuous – is distinguished by the natural renewal of soils by the spread of river silt.

Continuous and annual cultivation systems are relatively restricted in Africa and the most widespread technique is that of fallowing, with between two and twenty-five years when the land is unused. Such systems are found in both forest and savannah environments and periodically require the clearing of vegetation for new farms, usually by burning. In the case of forests, a good deal of effort is needed to fell trees prior to burning and in general the preparation of land after fallow periods requires large inputs of labour. But as forest-fallows are shortened the degradation of vegetation occurs, and grasses predominate as land is used more frequently. In grassland areas proper, clearing land for new farms is less difficult, but the weeding of crops becomes more demanding, as the amount of tree cover is reduced and the penetration of sunlight increased.

The fact that one can identify regions where different systems of cultivation are dominant does not mean that rural communities, or the constituent production units, are only using one system. Forest-fallow cultivators and even annual cultivators may still gather a wide range of foodstuffs, such as fruits, herbs and insects, which are an important part of their diet and which can assume a vital role when subsistence levels are threatened by poverty, indebtedness and poor harvests after lower than average rainfall. Also, farmers involved in continuous cropping may have some land which is under annual or short-fallow cultivation; the permutations are many and are frequently a reflection of the labour supply available, as well as the market prices for crops.

Most farmers try to grow as much as possible while minimizing risk and uncertainty. Risk may arise from voluntary or involuntary acts, such as the dependence on one or two crops, whereas uncertainty may come in the form of external factors such as drought, flood or changes in national and international farm prices. At a more local level, uncertainty may be related to unforeseen sickness, accidents or premature death within the farming household. Strategies to reduce risk and uncertainty may include different methods of organizing farm labour, the adoption of various crop combinations, or the manipulation of the micro-environment by techniques such as ridging, terracing and irrigation.

Another defence against uncertainty and risk is inter-cropping, which occurs in bush-fallow, short-grassland-fallow and annual cultivation systems. In Sierra Leone and Liberia, cassava is frequently planted with rice on upland bush-fallow rice farms, especially where sandy soils are dominant, and root crop is left over from one season to another, often into the fallow period, and becomes an insurance against poor yields of rice. In northern Nigeria inter-cropping of guinea corn, cowpeas and groundnuts is commonplace and the successive planting of these crops within a single growing season is rather like a 'collapsed' or shortened rotational system (Norman, 1974). In Kakamega District, Kenya, between 80 and 100 per cent of the maize area cultivated per household is intercropped with beans, cowpeas and millet; this proportion is particularly high because of the absence of commercial cash crops (Rukandema, 1978). However, commercial crops such as cotton and tobacco are usually grown in pure stands, a practice which was popularized and to some extent insisted upon by the colonial agricultural officers.

Mixed cropping does not produce the best yields per acre,

but in addition to security and a hedge against disaster it does give good returns to labour and some observers believe inter-cropping leads to greater production per unit of labour expended (Evans, 1960). The returns to labour, as opposed to returns to land, are an important aspect of household farming and a failure to appreciate this fact can lead to incorrect assessments of agricultural practice and performance. The mixture of crops in any one field, or indeed along any one ridge have frequently been misinterpreted; *un peu de tout* has been mistaken for *beaucoup de rien*. The returns to land and labour vary according to the farming systems used and the crops grown and the estimation of returns is by no means easy.

TIME SPENT ON FARM WORK

Measured on an annual basis, the time spent on farm work is relatively small throughout tropical Africa. According to an analysis of farm surveys undertaken by Cleave (1974), men spend between 530 and 2,135 hours per year on farm work with an average of 1,000 hours, compared with 3,000 hours for Egypt and Asia. In Africa the number of hours varies significantly from one farming system to another and in general arid regions have lower inputs because of shorter growing seasons, while in more humid areas of bush-fallowing land clearing and preparation takes up more time, which is further increased if perennial tree crops are grown. The presence of commercial crops can make significant differences; in the Nile Plains of Uganda it takes 188 man hour equivalents to produce an acre of mixed pigeon-peas, groundnuts and cassava, compared with 592 hours for cotton (Akenda-Ondoga, 1980). Also in the same area it was observed that soils affected labour inputs: sweet potatoes grown on the lighter valley soils of the Nile Plains needed 352 man hour equivalents per acre, compared with 494 on the heavier upland soils.

Although the hours spent on farming by Africans are low by international standards, one has to bear in mind that fallowing is widespread, man–land ratios are low and the combination of farm and non-farm work may be of a different order than in Asia or South America. One of the problems of studying African farming is that many rural dwellers combine farming with petty trading, crafts and domestic industry, in varying proportions which alter seasonally as well as from one year to another. Farm and non-farm work are both competing and conjunctive categories, and involvement in non-farm work is commonplace. Even at times of maximum use of family labour non-farm activities may continue; for example, Norman (1972) found that farmers spent 34 per cent of their time in off-farm employment during the peak month of farming activities. It may be that farmers who are all-year-round traders will forgo substantial short-term returns from farm work, as they get higher annual returns by trading throughout the year. On the other hand poorer farmers in the community may have to sell their labour in order to maintain subsistence levels during the 'hungry season', that is, during the period before the harvest, when their stocks of food may be at their lowest ebb or even non-existent. Seasonal variations in non-farm work are very pronounced and seem to be the norm; in Bunyole County, Uganda, only 11 per cent of a farming household's labour was devoted to non-farm work in the big rains (February to June); the proportion rose to 24 per cent in the little rains (mid-August to October) and then rose dramatically to 70 per cent in the slack season (Mwima-Mudeenya, 1978).

THE DIVISION OF LABOUR BY SEX AND AGE

The hours spent on farm work by women shows much more variation than for men. According to Cleave (1974), African women spend between 51 and 1,195 hours per year on farming, which reflects the relative importance of women as farmers in different regions, and the sexual division of labour among different societies. The importance of women as farmers has been recognized for some time (Baumann, 1928; Kaberry, 1952) although it has not been sufficiently taken into account by development planners. The role of women has been, and still is, crucial in the acceptance and success of new crops and crop species, because their introduction has repercussions on the organization and allocation of farm labour.

The study of work, agricultural or otherwise, makes little sociological sense without reference to the control and division of labour. Work is about material production *and* social transactions and the value of work may depend on the category of worker who performs it, which may rest upon distinctions of age, sex, caste or skill. The causes for the division of labour are not always plain or autonomous, and they are located within a complex of social, economic and political relationships. Specialization in its most extreme form may be by decree, and this most stringent definition would apply to job reservation under apartheid. A more common categorization is based on 'custom', especially the division between men's and women's work.

Throughout the sub-continent there is 'customary' sexual division of labour according to farming operations and crop-types; this primarily stems from socio-biological distinctions between heavy work, such as clearing and preparing farms, done by men, and lighter jobs, such as weeding and harvesting, done by women. Meillasoux distinguishes masculine processes (performed only by men), feminine processes (performed only by women), alternating processes (performed by men and women at certain stages and women at others), and mixed processes (where men and women work together at every stage) (Meillasoux, cited in Terray, 1972). But there are processes which are both mixed and alternating, for example, in the yam-cycle where men tie up plants, women weed and harvest, and both carry out the planting. Categorization of this kind is useful, but one must remember that the allocation of tasks does not always fit the norm; in the short run deviations occur through stress and illness and temporary absence, while in the long run new crops and prolonged absence may radically alter the allocation of jobs (De Schlippe, 1956).

The natural differences between the jobs men and women do are often heavily culturally determined and in addition may undergo sociological transformation to underwrite the dominance of one or other of the sexes (Wallman, 1979). Among some Muslims, such as the Hausa-Fulani of northern Nigeria, women are kept in seclusion (purdah) and contribute less than 5 per cent of the total farm labour. Seclusion here is a sign of economic status and, in the early twentieth century, with the decline of domestic slavery, former slave-women who had hitherto worked in the fields moved into seclusion, which changed the patterns of labour supply and sexual division of labour. But in some cases men have used sexual differentials to underwrite their own positions; this seems to be particularly true where new techniques and crops have been introduced which yield cash incomes (and the resources and goods they buy) and there seems to be a widespread, but not exclusive, division of labour, where women cultivate food staples and men cash crops.

In many cases the amount of farm work done by women may be less than by men, but if one includes other domestic work, such as food preparation and water carrying, then the hours of labour expended by women can increase dramatically. The economic roles of women are often underestimated, as they are subsumed in their status as wives. In Tanzania, Shapiro (1978; cited in Eicher and Baker, 1982) found that, although men spent more hours on farming than women, women worked 28 per cent more total hours per year on farming and non-farming activities compared with men. Furthermore, Shapiro discovered that women in his sampled households spent on average 90 minutes per day or 556 hours per year fetching water from wells scattered around the village. Shapiro was particularly interested in this aspect of women's work in view of the possibility of a centralized water system; he considered that even if the release of female labour occurred only at peak periods, then nearly 140 hours could be available for farm work or some other enterprise. In Burkina Faso (formerly Upper Volta), Barret *et al.* (1982) also found that men spent more time on farming than women, but, as in the Tanzania case, women worked more hours per year when other jobs and domestic chores were added. But it was apparent that where households had started using animal traction, the women worked significantly fewer hours than their counterparts using hand-hoe cultivation, while the difference in hours worked by men remained much the same.

It can be argued that the division of labour is not simply by custom, but arises from necessity as the patterns of farming change, new techniques are introduced and the household economy becomes restructured to meet new circumstances. As agriculture and the rural sector are integrated into the market economy, the farming of cash crops is not just a source of additional income for men, but a necessary part of the household economy for the payment of taxes and purchase of essential goods and services. Under such circumstances women's workloads may increase as they become more and more the producers of food staples, and this is a theme to which we will return in Chapters 3 and 4.

The amount and kinds of work women do may also be heavily influenced by men taking on increasing amounts of non-farm work, either locally or as migrant workers further afield. Non-farm work by men may be part of improving and maximizing household incomes, or it may stem again from the necessity of providing cash if opportunities are not available at home to produce agricultural surpluses from their own farms. In some areas farming households are effectively headed by women in the absence (either permanently or temporarily) of men. In Kenya, Staudt (1975) found, in a survey of 212 households, that 40 per cent were headed by females. In another part of Kenya, Rukandema (1978) found even higher proportions – 55 per cent – of females heading farming households. More often it is the younger males whose labour is diverted from farming, while older men remain as heads of farming households and they and the women provide the chief labour inputs. For example, in the Nile Province of Uganda male heads of household provided between 32 and 35 per cent of total farm labour, women between 34 and 40 per cent, but other adult males provided only between 11 and 17 per cent (Akenda-Ondoga, 1980).

The importance of women as farmers in Africa led Boserup (1970) to describe Africa as a 'region of female farming *par excellence*'. From selected surveys Boserup showed that women do more than half the agricultural work and in extreme cases as much as 70 and 80 per cent. In addition, in some parts of Africa, notably among the Yoruba and Ashanti, women play an important part as traders. Boserup has attempted to draw a general distinction between farming systems where men perform the majority of jobs, and those where women's work is predominant. This male-female dichotomy has been correlated with population density, technology and cultivation systems. For example, it is argued that under bush-fallow systems in low population density areas where root cultivation is practised, women usually perform a substantial part of the agricultural work compared with areas of cereal cultivation, where ploughs are more common, with men doing more work. In irrigated areas Boserup suggests that both men and women work hard. Furthermore, Boserup believes that it was the low labour inputs of men in forest-fallow systems which allowed African farmers to take advantage of opportunities offered by cash-crop farming in the nineteenth century and later European colonialists were able to induce or force underemployed men to become plantation workers, or small-scale producers of cash crops. Nothing was done to encourage the production of food staples, as these were primarily 'women's crops' and part of the accepted division of labour.

But the notion that men have traditionally stood outside the workforce in African agriculture is not true; as we have noted, in some Islamic areas women's work is restricted. Even where bush- or forest-fallows are common and cash crops minimal, men's inputs, for example, into yam and upland rice systems, are significant. The contention that shifting cultivation and hoe cultivation are distinguishing features of female systems overlooks the nature of the specific jobs involved in fallowing. The inputs of men may be limited in the number of hours, but the timing and effort required in clearing fallowed land is of critical importance to a successful season's farming. As Guyer (1984) has pointed out, the roots–cereal distinction ignores the differences within the categories. While women may provide most of the labour for roots, such as cassava, men's work is important in the cultivation of yams; similarly maize may be primarily grown by women, but men and women combine to cultivate rice, millet and sorghum.

The allocation of work according to age has not received as much attention as the sexual division of labour in African societies, perhaps because western-orientated observers are accustomed to thinking of children and the elderly as insignificant elements in the workforce (Schildkraut, 1979).

Labour inputs in farming are frequently calculated in terms of man-equivalents, where different values are allocated to men, women, children and the aged. For example, taking men of 15–64 years as 1.0, Norman (1972) counts children of 7–14 years as 0.5, men and women over 65 years as 0.5 and adult women of 15–64 years as 0.75. There are numerous methods of calculating man-equivalents but the difficulty is that all implicitly assume that performance rates are constant for all farm jobs, whereas women and children do some jobs, such as grading produce and certain types of weeding, better than men. Also the small amount of labour contributed by children may be undervalued, if it is applied at critical points in the cultivation cycle then the marginal productivity of their labour is very high.

The division of labour may of course be related to both age and sex; for example, only older women may do certain farm jobs, or have farms of their own. In Sierra Leone women have swamp rice farms, but only when they are middle-aged and past the point of rearing their last child. The distribution and size of women's rice plots may also be different from those of men; for example, in the Gambia they are smaller and closer to the compound, as this reduces time travelling to the fields, since farming has to be integrated with the other considerable duties of women within the household.

For both sexes the organization of farm work and the time spent in the fields may be influenced by the distance between the compound and the fields, which is a function of how the farm plots are distributed around the village. Time spent in travelling to the farm is not an insignificant part of labour-time in many peasant societies, although within any one community some farmers, according to their status, have farms much nearer than others. Absorption of time in travelling is much greater in areas where rural settlement is nucleated; for example, in the Zaria area of northern Nigeria about 161 hours out of a total of 1,173 hours worked by men were spent in travelling to their farms (Norman, 1972). Travelling is much less of a problem where settlements are dispersed and compounds are set within the plots that the household cultivates. This is a common pattern throughout East and Central Africa with the exception of the Shire Valley in Malawi, which has a nucleated population. Also in East and Central Africa farmland is frequently arranged in long narrow tracts, stretching from the hilltop down to the valley floor, with the compound set within this strip; such an arrangement gives each farming household a share of different types of terrain.

THE SUPPLY AND SEASONAL DISTRIBUTION OF LABOUR

Although there are islands of high population density in tropical Africa, for the most part the population is thinly scattered and the economy is more properly characterized as one of 'land surplus', in which labour is a limiting factor in production (Helleiner, 1966). The concepts of surplus labour and disguised unemployment derived from 'India-type' development models of the 1950s are not really applicable to Africa, with its low population densities and different institutional environments. Moreover, under conditions of hoe cultivation and seasonal rainfall the labour supply problem is intensified when bottlenecks occur in the farming cycle. At the local level, production units have to contend with limitations imposed by insufficient labour available from within households or kin-based groups, their ability to hire or borrow extra labour and whether institutionalized arrangements exist for communal village labour. Domestic groups also experience phases of expansion and contraction during their life-cycles, as well as being periodically debilitated by illness, accident and premature death. They may also face absence of members due to out-migration when the returns to agriculture are significantly less than for off-farm employment elsewhere. Under these conditions the two principal operational decisions facing many farmers are the *arduousness* of jobs, and their *urgency*. Arduous jobs demand male labour, whereas urgency is a matter of correct timing and the completion of jobs within a seasonally-patterned cultivation cycle. All farmers face the problems of seasonality, but the means whereby rich and poor farmers cope with them are different. We shall return to this issue later; for the moment we will look at the basic problems of labour use and seasonal farming.

Throughout tropical Africa it is the amount, duration, incidence and reliability of rainfall which pose the main problem for the agriculturalist, as temperatures are generally high enough to sustain plant growth throughout the year. Therefore, the length of the growing season is closely related to seasonal rainfall and agriculture is confined to the wet season, unless water-control systems are available to allow farming to continue throughout the dry season. Apart from irrigation schemes based on barrages and dams, there are few parts of tropical Africa where indigenous farmers have practised irrigated farming. Seasonal rainfall is experienced in both forests and grasslands, but it is particularly pronounced in the savannah areas, which contain some 70 per cent of the population of tropical Africa. The distinction between forest and savannah is a basic one, and from an agricultural point of view the distinction lies not only in the staples grown – root and tree crops in the forest and grain crops in the savannah – but in the length of growing season, the reliability of cultivation and the effort needed for successful farming.

Variations in the onset of the rains may be of great significance for the clearing of land, for example, where forest and low bush have to be cut and burnt for shifting cultivation, or rotational bush-fallowing. While some farmers always leave clearing too late, abnormally early rains can inhibit the burning of new plots over wide areas. But in the savannah grasslands, where rainfall totals are below 40 inches (1,000 mm), the incidence and duration of rainfall can be particularly critical. If after a long dry season of some seven months or more, the rains come in short fierce downpours, then the run-off is fast, the chance of erosion greater and the effectiveness of rainfall is reduced. The same amount of rainfall coming in different 'packages' can have quite different results. In north-western Nigeria, 40 inches (1,000 mm) of ill-distributed rainfall have produced floods and poor harvests, while only 16 inches (400 mm) of well-distributed rain have produced excellent crops of millet.

When farming is restricted to the wet season, there is an uneven spread of farm workloads and it is the *flow* not just the *stock* of labour which is of importance. Frequently the size of farms is directly related to the labour force available at peak periods of activity in the cultivation cycle, and bottlenecks in the labour supply are of crucial importance for African farmers. In essence, the timing of specific agricultural operations can be critical, and need to be carried out over short periods of time to achieve good yields. Labour inputs can vary significantly from day to day during the cultivation cycle, and the length of working day may depend on whether 'arduousness' or 'urgency' is demanded. In Sierra Leone, upland rice cultivation accounts for approximately half of the rice produced, which is of the order of 400,000m tons per annum. Upland rice cultivation is by means of rotational bush-fallowing and length of fallow tends to vary directly with soils and rainfall, and inversely with population densities and the size of farming households. For the country as a whole, 38.7 per cent of upland farms have a fallow period of seven to nine years (Njoku and Karr, 1973). The length of fallow affects labour require-

Table 1.1 *Upland rice farms, Njala, Sierra Leone, 1970: average workdays per acre and percentage of hired labour*

	Job (male/female/children)	Average workdays per acre		Percentage hired labour	
Preparing	Brushing (m)	8.7	21.5	10	24
	Felling (m)	6.4		7	
	Burning and clearing (m)	6.4		7	
Planting	Ploughing (m)	10.0	19.3	4	10
	Harrowing (m + f)	9.3		6	
Tending	Weeding (f)	20.4		<1	<1
	Bird scaring (ch)	n.a.		n.a.	
	Harvesting (m + f)	n.a.		n.a.	

Source: Njoku and Karr (1973).

ments, and where bush has been allowed to regenerate over a long period of time a correspondingly greater effort is needed to clear and prepare it for cultivation.

The farming of upland rice can be divided into four basic components. First, preparation, which includes brushing (cutting undergrowth), felling trees, burning and clearing rubbish; second, planting by spreading seed in broadcast fashion and covering it by hoeing; third, weeding; and finally harvesting. The jobs are divided between the sexes; preparation is done by men, planting by both sexes, weeding by women, and harvesting by both sexes. Table 1.1 shows the average workdays per acre for preparing, planting and weeding upland rice in three villages studied by Njoku and Karr (1973). The complementarity of jobs between the sexes is quite apparent, but the cultivation cycle is started by large inputs of male labour for brushing and felling, which means enough men must be available before the rains begin and hinder burning. Off-farm employment in the dry season may have adverse effects on upland rice farming, and the development of indigenous diamond mining along the rivers of Sierra Leone at low water in the dry season has tended to divert or delay the return of men to clear farms. Significantly, of all jobs on the farm, it was preparation which used most hired labour, usually provided by local or migrant workers.

The marginal productivity of labour can be very high at certain times in the farming cycle, and numerous studies have shown that improved returns stem from quite small applications of labour, for example, during weeding and harvesting. Therefore one of the objectives of many farmers is an adequate strategy for coping with structural and geographical imperfections in the farm-labour supply. Studies undertaken in Senegal and the Gambia have shown the wide differences in returns from groundnuts planted in the early and late season (Tourtre, 1954; Haswell, 1953). In Senegal, it has been estimated that for every day's delay in planting there is a 2 per cent fall in yield; while in the Gambia yields of 663 lbs per acre were obtained from early-planted well-weeded plots, compared with 304 lbs from late-sown and little-weeded plots. But Haswell also found that, even for the later-planted crop, adequate and correctly-timed weeding substantially improved the yields of groundnuts. Groundnuts are integrated with other crops, which means that farm work is phased throughout the growing season in response to the number of crops grown and their specific requirements.

When food staples are integrated with crops such as groundnuts and cotton which are grown primarily for the market, allocation of labour and bottlenecks in the supply may become particularly difficult, and this is an issue we shall return to later. But even when cash crops make up a small part of the farming system, the stock and flow of labour can still act as constraints on achieving adequate outputs. Rukandema's investigation of small-scale farms in the Kakamega District of Kenya gives some insights into labour allocation where farmers are primarily growing maize inter-cropped with beans, cowpeas and millet. The demand for labour is particularly strong from March to May: what can be done then determines the success of other activities which are to follow. Between 43 and 45 per cent of total labour inputs are used in this and about three-quarters of the labour expended per acre is used on seedbed preparation and weeding. It is not, apparently, competition from other crops which poses the problem, but the competition among different operations required in the cultivation of one crop. Preparation, planting and weeding overlap and by the fourth week in March competition is very intense; by mid-May the crisis is over and all work is confined to weeding (Fig. 1.1).

One important feature of farming in Kakamega is the staggered planting of maize, and Rukandema speculated on the reasons for this strategy, which he subsumes under three types. First, some observers, such as Clayton (1968), think this practice is a reaction to uncertain rainfall: small plots prepared successively, rather than one large plot, help to reduce risks of failure should the rains be too light or too heavy; in other words, staggered planting allows continuous adjustment. Second, others such as Cleave (1974) and Von Rotenhan (1968) believe that staggering is a means of overcoming labour bottlenecks and avoiding clashes such as those experienced in Kakamega, by stretching the workload. Thirdly, staggering may be used to spread the harvest and achieve a more continuous food supply. In Rukandema's opinion, the third option only applies where the range of crops is considerable. The second category appeared to apply in one area where there was a good deal

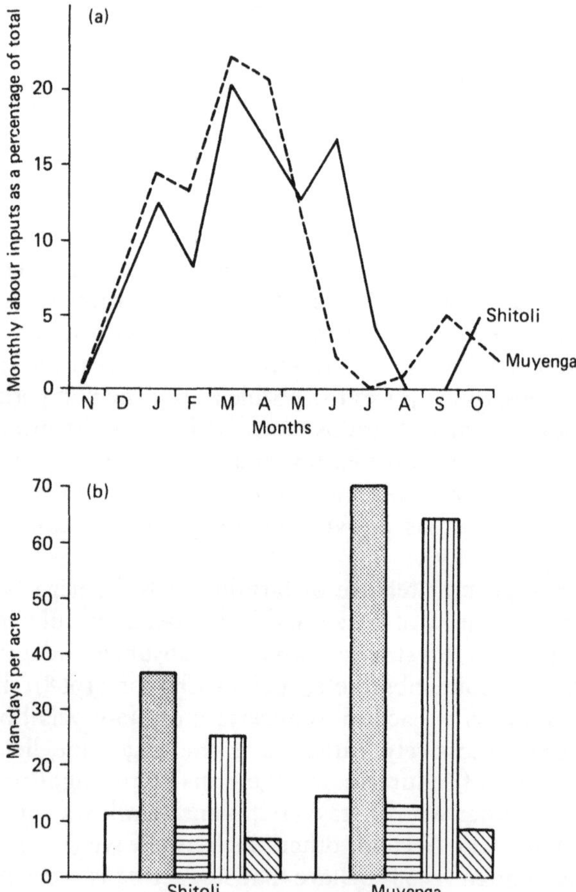

Fig. 1.1 The seasonal distribution of labour for maize cultivation in Kakamega District, Kenya. (a) Seasonal distribution of labour for the cultivation of maize. (b) Distribution of labour according to jobs for the cultivation of maize. (c) Labour use in maize cultivation in seven-day periods, March–May.

Source: Rukandema (1978).

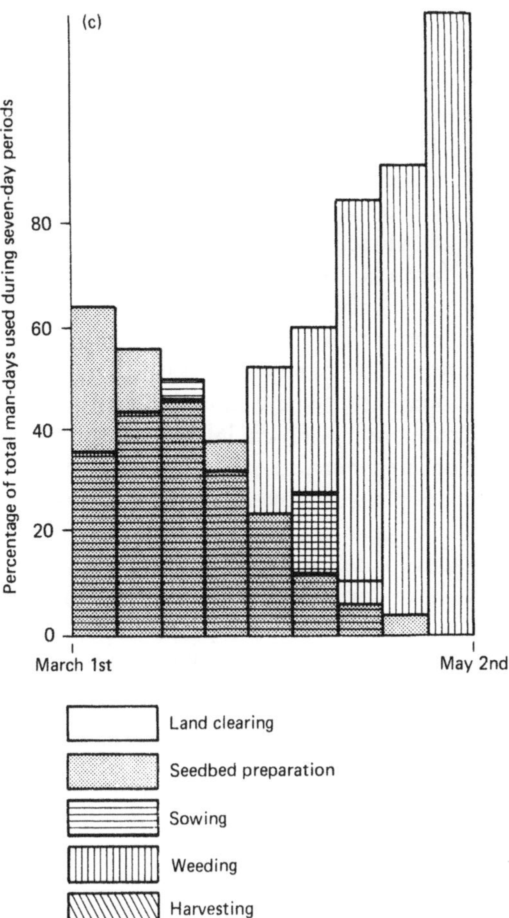
(c)
Percentage of total man-days used during seven-day periods
0
20
40
60
80
March 1st
May 2nd
Land clearing
Seedbed preparation
Sowing
Weeding
Harvesting

of out-migration and no ox-ploughs, but in general the first category seemed most applicable. On the other hand, this risk-reducing strategy reduces yields, because the jobs are not all done at the optimum time, and in some cases it actually produces bottlenecks in the labour supply. It would appear that farmers have to trade off disadvantage against advantage and arrive at some compromise.

There is, of course, a way out of labour shortages, at least for some farmers, and that is by hiring labour. In Kakamega, hired labour forms between 12 and 19 per cent of the total labour input, a relatively small proportion, and is used almost exclusively on seedbed preparation and weeding. Apparently, where man–land ratios are high the marginal productivity of local labour is quite low; there is a tendency for men here to sell labour to areas with low population densities and overall shortages. But it is not just simply a question of the transfer of labour from areas of surplus to areas of deficit, from those who have too much to those who have too little; it is need combined with the ability to pay and extract surpluses. One of the shortcomings of the labour profiles to which we have referred is that they are aggregates for either villages or for sets of households within one village, and they hide the variations in household size, power, wealth, crop performances, and alternative sources of income. The labour peaks in the profiles, while identifying a general problem, do not tell us whether some, most or all households are experiencing difficulties in finding an adequate supply of labour.

In the Kenya villages investigated by Rukandema there were households who were selling labour in the wet season when the demand was at its greatest, because they were experiencing the effects of the 'hungry season'. This was when domestic food supplies were at their lowest, and men left the farm to earn money as labourers to meet immediate food requirements; these were usually the poorest families within the community. The hungry season is an important aspect of seasonality in African farming, and it seriously affects the efficiency of labour, yet it has not received as much attention as it deserves; it also highlights the differential in well-being which exists within many villages.

THE HUNGRY SEASON

As we have seen, it is towards the end of the dry season that work has to begin on clearing and preparing the ground for wet-season crops. But it is also the time when water becomes scarce and drawing and fetching water for human and animal consumption increases energy and labour requirements. Poorer members of the community have less land and limited means for organizing adequate labour supplies; they have less food, because less was grown last season, yet their future food supplies depend on the correct timings of inputs, chiefly of labour. Faced with negative energy balances, the options are to borrow money or inputs from richer members of the community, or to seek daily-paid work to buy in food.

Women are particularly at risk during the hungry season, as their workloads rise on the farm and births peak at this period. Anticipating hard work, mothers tend to terminate breast feeding, or if they continue the food level is reduced as diets become poorer. The wet season is a period when malaria, diarrhoea and skin infections peak, and for everyone illness affects the timing, efficiency and availability of farm work; but it bears heavily on the poorer people who move into situations of dependency involving kin, neighbours, or money lenders, a situation from which they may not escape. In areas where land sales are increasing, and communal tenure weakening, it is precisely in periods of crisis, such as the hungry season, that distressed farmers may have finally to resort to sale of land, and become landless workers. Dependency and subordination pass down the line from the rich to the poor, from men to women, children and the aged. Eventually harvest-time brings relief, and mortality and morbidity decline as the quantity of food increases; ceremonies such as marriages take place, the peak in conception occurs and the cycle begins again.

The scenario sketched here derives from a conference on the seasonal dimensions of poverty, which was analysed by Chambers, Longhurst, Bradley and Feachem (1979). The authors stress under-perception of the problem by urban-based researchers and agricultural officers, who often focus exclusively on farming practice and who find it difficult to travel in rural areas in the wet season; certainly it is a time when farmers are least available. Nor do farmers seek even the limited medical facilities available, as they are busy and access to clinics is difficult. The impact of the hungry season affects many farmers, but some qualifications are required; for example, in Muslim areas women may be less disadvantaged if they do not fully engage in farm work. Also, off-farm income may be very important as a smoothing device, and better still if it is dry-season employment, which can be used to build up cash-reserves, whereas wet-season employment exacerbates the labour-supply problem.

Climate is less the cause of rural distress and poverty and more a context in which poverty can be sustained and deepened through the exploitation of the poor by the rich. The seasonal rhythm of farming does allow the possibility of recovery, but a prolonged failure of the rains, or erratic climate conditions over a period of time may be of more significance. As Chambers *et al.* (1979) point out, successive bad seasons may have a 'ratchet' effect, which presses downwards, fron which recovery becomes almost impossible. The practical implication of a better understanding of the hungry season and of seasonal farming is to make sure that they are built into rural planning schemes, and to affirm the links between agricultural activity, nutrition, health and food prices. Public health measures should certainly take account of the peaks of infection and workloads, and perhaps it might be possible to examine the possibility of communal child care when women are most occupied. But one issue well worth thinking about is the improvement of food storage in villages; cheap and efficient food storage might do a lot more good than the distribution of food-aid.

SUMMARY

The workloads of African farmers are shaped by their cultivation systems and seasonal climates, which in some places restricts the growing season to as little as five months. Farm work becomes uneven because of the alternation of wet and dry season, and intense periods of activity can be followed by relative inactivity. In areas of low population density the supply and distribution of labour can be a major preoccupation of farmers and the value of work done is materially affected by its correct timing. Patterns of consumption also have a seasonal component if farmers grow the bulk of their own food, and serious shortfalls in the hungry season can be the result of either labour shortages or lateness in finishing farm work in the run-up to harvest. But if farm work is about material production and technology, it is also about social transactions. The control of nature is also about the control of one person, or category of persons, over another and their access to resources and benefits (Wallman, 1979). Farming demands the organization and control of labour and methods of distributing the product. In the next chapter we begin to look at the organizing principles around which production units can be built.

2

DOMESTIC GROUPS AND THE ORGANIZATION OF FARM LABOUR

The domestic group provides a focal point for agricultural production, where age, sex and kin act as *traditional* determinants of who does what, who is dependent on whom and what are the rewards for one's labour. It is also the place where age and sex intersect through marriage, which is a key to internal differentiation, a sign of adulthood and the route to semi- or ultimate independence through access to resources such as land and labour (La Fontaine, 1978). The control of marriage can be of particular importance, as access to women is an integral part of the reproduction of domestic groups; women are not only producers, but producers of producers.

Domestic groups are not easily defined, and while residence patterns provide a basic index of their internal boundaries and internal structure, these characteristics spring from primary factors of kinship, descent, marriage and economic co-operation aimed at the groups' sustenance and reproduction. The fact that domestic groups undergo cycles of development, fission and decay also affects their composition and structure. While a 'nuclear family' may be identical with a domestic group, more frequently it is a term used to include several generations, as well as collaterals and even adopted members. In Forte's words, 'it is a domestic domain of kin, descent and other jural and affectional bonds' (Fortes, 1958).

Domestic groups provide a pivotal element for the organization of agricultural production, and while a domestic group may be both a unit of production and of consumption, alternatively it may divide into two or more production groups or teams, who may re-unite for joint-consumption. But joint-production and consumption may only operate for some farming activities, such as the production of food staples, whereas commercial farming and non-farm activities may be undertaken by sub-groups, who wholly or in part receive the product of their labour. In terms of agricultural production, the organization of farming groups and sub-groups may display considerable flexibility, a feature which is more important than 'boundedness'. The ability of agricultural production units to form and re-form is important in the context of seasonal agriculture, as well as of environmental hazards and economic uncertainty. The domestic group's efforts at production and reproduction may mean that in different circumstances it draws upon more distant kin, or subdivides into elementary families; such changes may result from short-term internal pressures or from more profound structural changes which are external to the group. The intention of this chapter is to look at examples of how age, sex and kin act as traditional determinants of agricultural production within the context of the domestic group. We shall examine lineages and joint-families as methods of organizing agricultural production, and subsequently use these as benchmarks from which to assess the changes which have, and are, taking place in the use and organization of farm labour in Africa.

The lineage, or lineage segment, provides one basic model for the organization of a cluster of households which is controlled by an elder with whom the households identify through ties of blood or kinship. Segmentary lineages are characteristic of acephalous peoples who have not been incorporated into larger states and who have a strong sense of territoriality and communality of land ownership. On the other hand there are regions of tropical Africa where states and commercial trading have been the norm for several hundred years. For example, the Sudanic belt of West Africa has seen the rise and fall of several pre-colonial states reaching back to the eighth century, which had urban systems and a well-developed social division of labour. Farmers were also traders and craftsmen, while those who were specialized in certain skills formed specific castes of workers. The Sudanic states were financed by complex systems of taxation, and slavery was widespread as a means of organizing and controlling labour, not least agricultural labour on plantations, and in domestic groups. Under such conditions age, sex and kin were part of a larger matrix of economic, social and political institutions, and the model of domestic production and reproduction hinged more on joint-families than on lineages, except in the case of chiefs and rulers.

In geographically- and economically-remoter areas, descent and kinship may still form the core of domestic production, while in areas such as commercial crop zones and urban peripheries pre-capitalist forms have been severely eroded as market relations have become dominant. Therefore in specific places and instances the influence of kinship and the extended family varies, operating for some purposes, such as the production of food staples, but not for others, such as growing commercial crops. It is also possible that the reliance on kinship and the extended family varies according to the relative wealth and position of production units, while in times of crisis or economic distress the proportions of kin and non-kin labour may vary.

Marxist anthropologists have been particularly concerned with the structures of pre-capitalist societies and how they *have* been, and *are* being transformed through their incorporation into the international capitalist economy. In this respect Meillasoux's work on the Gouro of the Ivory Coast is now generally accepted as one of the turning-points in economic anthropology (Meillasoux, 1964). Marxist analyses of pre-capitalist formations are by means of the modes of production which characterize them, and several modes have emerged in an attempt to identify the African 'case' and its historical development. Defining modes of production and their articulation has proved to be a contentious issue and it is arguable that it has generated more heat than light. A mode of production is generally taken to comprise two elements: the forces of production (land, labour force, tools, raw materials) and the social relations of production, that is, the patterns of co-operation of the people involved in the exploitation of these forces, together with the division of the product.

In the context of agricultural production and farm labour, the mode of production analysis looks not only at sets of people who live, eat and farm together, but at the social relationships which bind them. As Terray (1972) observes, production units are agents of production whose dimensions and structure are determined both by the forces of production and the relations of production. Each unit is characterized by the way it combines the factors of production in specific quantities (land, labour, capital) and by the social relationships between the constituent parts of the unit. In other words, there are the technical problems of growing a crop or crops by using particular cultivation systems, which are operated by sets of workers defined not only according to their size and composition, but by their forms of co-operation. Once the co-operation of individuals is demanded by the job, then there must be control and organization of work and division of labour. The relations of production also determine how the produce is distributed, as well as the structure of consumption units, although this does not mean that consumption and production units necessarily coincide.

Questions about who is working for whom and with whom and how the product of labour is distributed lead to questions about associated forms of hierarchy and subordination, as well as those about reciprocity, and internal and external exchange. In the view of Meillasoux (1964; 1972), it is the investigation of economic relations which leads on to the understanding of kinship, politics and ideology and the way in which these play their part in the reproduction and continuation of domestic groups. The concept of production can be extended to include the production of people as well as goods, and the control of the means of human reproduction (i.e. the distribution of wives) may be of more importance than the control of the material means of production.

The social relationships involved in work invite considerations about the relationships between elders and juniors, matrimonial exchanges, questions of control of labour and resources, and stratification within the segmentary-based production units and in the larger village community. A central issue for Marxist anthropologists (and others) is that lineage and kinship in pre-capitalist societies are distinguishing features of the organization of production, and that rank and status are strongly constrained by birth; where there is some disagreement is the extent to which kinship, ideology and political relations (superstructure) dominate social relations and their reproduction, and whether in the last instance it is the economic base which is determinate.

Lineage segments and joint-families are used in the remainder of this chapter to explore methods of organizing farm labour as part of the general process of production and reproduction. In doing so, we shall pay particular attention to the redistribution of labour within and among domestic groups as they strive to maintain cohesiveness and viability. On the other hand there are contrary forces which lead to the splitting of groups; lineages segment, joint-families are susceptible to fission and cycles of development and decay. The models we discuss here are intended primarily as baselines from which subsequent chapters and issues can proceed as we look at the shift towards individuation, and the use of hired labour. Our discussion uses three specific pieces of ethnographic research to examine lineage and joint-families: the study of the Gouro in the Ivory Coast by Meillasoux (1964), the account by Goody (1958) of the LoDagaba in Ghana and the investigation of the Soninké in Mali by Pollet and Winter (1971).

KINSHIP AND DESCENT AND THE ORGANIZATION OF FARM LABOUR

In Africa, social units have often been defined as a number of individuals of both sexes, linked by descent or kinship, who are grouped territorially under the authority of a head-man. Such social groupings are largely (although not exclusively) self-sustaining, having communal ownership of land and operating labour-intensive farming based on simple technology. However, although the individual means of production may be simple, the production techniques employed by the group may be complex; division of labour is according to age and sex, while the circulation of foodstuffs is organized by and centred on a hierarchy of senior members. Women work for and with their husbands, who hand over the produce as appropriate to senior members of the group, who organize labour and provide food, thus establishing a two-way circulation of goods, upwards and downwards, which creates a chain of dependent relationships.

The nature of authority and dependence is of some

importance in understanding the workings of domestic groups and entails the links established through lineage or kinship. Kinship is not necessarily a genetic concept since systems are so varied and include those who are adopted as well as fictive relationships, and it cannot be assumed that fatherhood is the same thing as *genitor*. Kinship expresses relationships which form the basis of social cohesion, and it may be better to speak of social kinship, which is built on economic relationships. As we have noted, the means of production are relatively simple, therefore they cannot be used by a particular group to control producers; the means of production are basically tools and land, the latter being communally 'owned' wherever use-rights are the norm. On the other hand skills can assume a complex part of production techniques and give authority, for example, as 'one who knows'. The acquisition of knowledge, which may involve custom, history and the ritual necessary for the functioning of society, comes with time and age and goes beyond the fundamentals of subsistence. Thus age and seniority become important attributes, which lead to control and dependence.

But in labour-intensive agriculture it is the access to and organization of labour which is often important and, although this may arise in numerous ways, the control over women can be paramount. Although control over granaries and the redistribution of food legitimizes the authority of seniors, both food and knowledge perish and juniors eventually acquire knowledge. A young man may be able to get tools and satisfy his basic needs, but this leaves him with little scope for manoeuvre because he requires dependants if he is to succeed economically or socially. Dependants are the means of recreating the social models from which he comes, and he needs to take a wife and beget children to become an effective social and economic unit, as well as acquiring status and a share in the communal life of the group and the village community which lies beyond it. But seniors control wives, and in an economy where production is labour-intensive, then the control of the 'producers of producers' is vital.

The control of marriage transactions is a basic form of relation with other domestic groups and communities, since at any given point in time there may be a lack of marriageable women available, therefore search procedures become necessary. Also, those who give a girl in marriage expect to receive one in return, but immediate reciprocity is not possible because of the distribution of females and their ages within domestic groups. Consequently organizing marriage involves entering into time-bargains regulated by dowry and bridewealth. Only those who can guarantee the return of women can enter into marriage deals, which is something reserved for the elders within the group. The arrangement of marriages is much easier if the group is large, as less gaps occur in the age-range of marriageable women; but large groups are not equally easy to manage for the purposes of farming. Therefore domestic groups may be large for the purposes of consumption and control of reproduction, but they frequently subdivide into constituent production units. In other words, segmentation into sub-groups occurs at the economic level, while cohesiveness is maintained at the level of an exogamic enlarged cell.

The structural reproduction of the unit demographically needs an opening-out and thus it is in this sphere, of dealing with the external world, that elders become significant. Endogamy is rarely the rule in agricultural societies, except for aristocratic lineages, as marriage within the group would threaten seniority. The organization of marriage is not just a means of securing wives, but involves strategies related to the correction of imbalances which occur due to illness, accident, premature death and differential fecundity. Therefore, the social reproduction of the group is not simply a natural process, but one of management and political endeavour, which needs the authority of elders. The elder acts as a foster-father to all those junior to him, in the sense that the father is he who feeds you, and has claim to your labour and its product; and, as the regulator of social reproduction, the father is he who marries you. As we have already noted, the concept of an elder, or father should not be confused with genitor, and kinship extends beyond natural relations expressed through procreation, and hierarchical relationships and dependence among brothers.

Most of the foregoing remarks derive from Meillasoux's study of the Gouro in the Ivory Coast; his analysis of agricultural production is particularly interesting, as it gives a valuable perspective on how segmentary lineage-based societies ideally organize their farm labour. The Gouro are concerned primarily with the production of food staples, using rotational bush-fallow techniques, and there are varying degrees of co-operation in the production of rice, yams, plantains, vegetables and manioc, which in Meillasoux's words form a hierarchy of foodstuffs, with the major emphasis on rice and yams. Food is the basic concern and the collective meal taken twice daily brings together the members of domestic groups, which are constructed around a lineage or segment of a lineage. As Meillasoux demonstrates, the genealogical relationships form a pattern, or model, around which productive relationships are built, yet endlessly modified and renewed. The collective meal is the end-product of the process of agricultural co-operation in which both productive and non-productive members share.

In many instances the lineage segment comprises both the unit of production and consumption under the control of its head, but larger segments may be broken into sub-segments for the purpose of farming. For example, a father and his sons, or a senior brother and his juniors, may each head a farm production unit or team in which they have control of

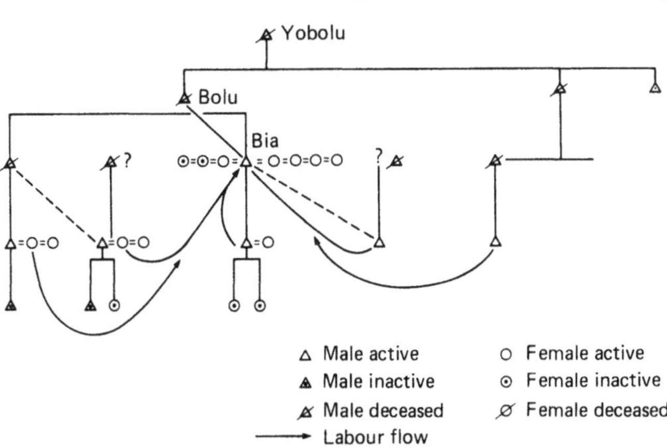

Fig. 2.1 The organization of farm labour within a lineage sub-segment.
Source: Meillasoux (1964).

the labour of their wives and married sons, and their wives and unmarried children (Fig. 2.1). But it is the elder (father or senior brother) who presides over the collective consumption of the group and who controls granaries and marriages. However, as the diagram in Figure 2.1 shows, farming units may be organized outside, or beyond, the strict genealogical model, because there has to be re-distribution of labour to correct imbalances which develop over time.

In the example given in Figure 2.1, although the production units are centred on three sub-segments, they include transfers of labour from one to another as well as embracing adopted members whose descent is uncertain. This re-distribution of labour is a necessary part of making effective work units by manufacturing a balance of active and non-active members. Also, differential mortality within the group creates problems, and for example, on the death of an elder, re-grouping of labour occurs towards his successor, or, if a junior, towards one's senior. Differential fecundity and accidents also disturb the age–sex distribution and dependency relations between producers and non-producers which have to be adjusted. Children may be shuffled around among classificatory fathers, while adoption of strangers may also take place, provided they become dependent workers. Therefore we are faced with functional groups whose members are associated by economic relations, especially through their labour, in the production of food, rather than through strict consanguinity or biological relationships. As we have noted before, kinship must be flexible enough to accommodate these strategies.

DOMESTIC GROUPS AND DEVELOPMENT CYCLES

Meillasoux's study of the Gouro is concerned to stress the importance of continuity and the elements of anteriority and posteriority – those who come before and after. But the composition of domestic groups changes over time and developmental cycles are of some importance in the productive process. Fortes (1958) and Goody (1958) have discussed at length the dynamics of domestic groups centred on joint-families, but their concern is neither with genealogical cleavage or segmentation, where internal subdivision takes place while the group maintains cohesion, nor with complete fission, such as in the break-up of a marital unit, but with fission of a cyclical nature (Goody, 1958). Domestic groups are ephemeral and, notwithstanding their relations with ancestors, they undergo a continuous process of growth, fission and sometimes decay, dependent on the three-generational cycle of human life and the consequent establishment, growth and dispersal of conjugal residential units.

Goody's work among the Tallensi and LoDagaba of Ghana led him to make a distinction between domestic groups based upon reproduction and those based on production. By 'reproduction' he means demographic reproduction, when the elementary family is paramount, whereas in production the joint-family is a group of people who act together in the production of food, its distribution, preparation and consumption. The farming groups comprise those males who farm, harvest and store the main crops jointly with the women and children they support. Compared with Meillasoux's work on the Gouro, for Goody production and consumption units are the same and it is not the control of grain and its distribution which secures the cohesion of groups. But Goody did look at the kinship relationships between adult males and their relationships with senior members. He posits two modal types which are found in all patrilineal agricultural societies; the first is a fraternal grouping of full siblings, the second, paternal groups comprising father and sons; similar groupings have been recognized by numerous workers among the Hausa-Fulani of northern Nigeria (Smith, 1955; Hill, 1972; Goddard *et al.*, 1971). But such groups are not stable; at some point hiving-off occurs to form other types of group, and it is how and when this fission occurs within the limits of a three-generational development cycle that interests Goody. Goody believes that fission occurs at different times in different groups because of variations in property relations, and he confronts alternative explanations which are based on different systems of production, or variations in ecology.

Goody focussed his attention on two groups in northern Ghana, the LoDagaba and the LoWiili. The LoDagaba cultivate more extensive areas, practising rotational-fallowing, and make bush farms, while the LoWiili have a more continuous system of cultivation and a greater use of manure. But apparently the different farming systems do not demand any major differences in productive relations; rights in land, the crops and tools used, are all similar. On the other hand communal farming is more apparent where rotational bush-fallowing is practised, as the more arduous work of clearing bush requires co-operation. It might be expected therefore that production units would be larger among the LoDagaba, but this turns out not to be the case; in fact groups tend to be smaller.

Among the LoWiili, who practise predominantly continuous cropping, 60 per cent of units were joint ones, that is, more than one adult male, while the corresponding proportion for the LoDagaba was 27 per cent. This means that in developmental terms fission occurs at an earlier stage among the shifting cultivators (LoDagaba), than among continuous cultivators (LoWiili). In both cases each individual *begins* farming with a father or elder brother, but the smaller groups among the LoDagaba indicate that fission occurs earlier in the developmental cycle of a domestic group. The LoWiili show a wider genealogical span in their production units, while among the LoDagaba there were only two types: a man and his sons, and a man and a full brother. Fission occurs at an early stage among paternal units, as eldest sons break away at an early age, and in fraternal units there is similarly an early break. It will be apparent from this account that the incidence and composition of joint-units must be viewed in the context of a developmental cycle, as part of a process, otherwise a good deal of spurious analysis can arise, chiefly as a result of static, cross-sectional analyses of domestic groups at a particular point in time. Indeed, this emphasizes the care needed in identifying groups as nuclear families, or extended families, as they are not static, but pass through stages of growth, decay and renewal and can assume both forms at different times in their developmental cycle.

But why were there differences in the size of domestic

groups between the LoWiili and the LoDagaba? As we have seen, Goody did not see it as a distinction between bush-fallowing and continuous cultivation, nor was it explained by differences in age structure, and the age of marriage in the two groups. The reason advanced by Goody lies in property relations; and matrilineal inheritance of wealth among the LoDagaba is primarily the cause of earlier fission. The tendency is for fathers to oust their senior sons for their own good, while keeping the juniors. On the death of the father his wealth is inherited primarily through the matriclan (for example, his nephews), which therefore weakens links between a man and his eldest sons. The juniors tend to stay on as a prop for the father's old age, and in turn they receive extra gifts and control of the granary on their father's death.

The organization and allocation of work is affected according to inheritance systems, and, for example, reciprocal labour is common among the LoWiili (patrilineal), the only non-reciprocal labour being that provided for a future wife's father. But among the LoDagaba (matrilineal) a man is expected by his mother's brother to bring hoeing parties, because not only does he ultimately inherit from his uncle, but the uncle provides the bride-price for a second wife (he also receives half-bride-price for his sister's daughter). Therefore, a man, especially a senior brother, may spend more time on his uncle's farm than on his father's, which increases the tendency to hive-off and form his own farming household. It was Goody's conclusion that fission occurred earlier, and groups were smaller, among the LoDagaba compared with the LoWiili, chiefly because of different systems of property relations and inheritance. So the difference between patrilineal and matrilineal systems adds another dimension to the discussion of the domestic production unit, as well as the general concept of a developmental cycle applicable to all groups. But production is only one side of the coin; as Meillasoux has demonstrated, distribution and consumption of the product can be a vital element in the structuring of domestic production groups. How do the LoDagaba and LoWiili perform in this respect?

The LoDagaba women are much less dependent on their husbands than their counterparts among the LoWiili; the former have much larger quantities of grain at their disposal and may have their own granary. In addition, LoDagaba women have food supplies which do not derive from their husbands. On marriage a girl receives goods from her mother and her mother's brothers. Nothing is received from fathers, but at each guinea-corn harvest women return to help their fathers with the harvest, and they take a certain amount of corn, which is how they acquire grain outside their husbands' domain. The grain may be used for sale or for beer-making; the extent of trading in grain may depend on whether a woman has a son's wife to do domestic duties, in order to give her time for trading. Thus we see another flow of farm labour; this time it is from a wife to her father, which may involve movements outside the village, as well as the domestic production unit.

But why do LoDagaba women have control over larger amounts of grain? The smaller production units have been explained by the fact that, although production is built around the patriclan, the inheritance of wealth, that is, the surplus of production over consumption, is vested in the matriclan. When a man dies, all immovable objects such as farms, implements, houses and shrines pass to agnatic kinsmen. But movable objects such as cattle and money pass to his uterine kinsmen (nephews). Livestock and cash come from the sale of grain, and therefore what is left in the granary technically must also be included. The situation is acute when a man is the last brother, because then his property goes to his sister's son (nephew). While a good man would always leave grain to support his widow until the next harvest, not all men display this virtue, therefore a husband is expected to hand over large amounts of grain to a wife as an insurance and protection against such an event.

Among the LoDagaba the unit of consumption is a *matrisegment* whereas production is centred on a *patrisegment*, to which women also contribute their labour. Cooking units only occur *within* farming units, but they do not necessarily correspond to them in terms of membership in the way the wives of co-brothers who form a fraternal farming unit do. A young wife may cook with her mother-in-law but not for a co-wife once they both have children eating solid food; what really divides wives into separate cooking units is the distribution of food among children. A cooking group splits when the second wife begins to wean her first child. It was Goody's conclusion from his work among the LoDagaba that internal differentiation of the production unit is in the severality of cooking units; which is a different situation from that encountered among the Gouro by Meillasoux, where the communality was dictated by the control of the granary by an elder; although several hearths were formed, the meals were for the whole domestic unit, which was differentiated. Cohesion was maintained by the circulation of food within the segment or sub-segment of a lineage.

DAILY AND WEEKLY VARIATIONS IN THE ORGANIZATION OF FARM LABOUR

The cases examined so far have stressed the social relations of production and distribution, and how units of production and consumption change over time. Some work done by Pollet and Winter (1971) among the Soninké of the Upper Niger basin reinforces these ideas, but also gives more detailed insights into labour flows and organization over shorter periods of time, such as a day, and thereby

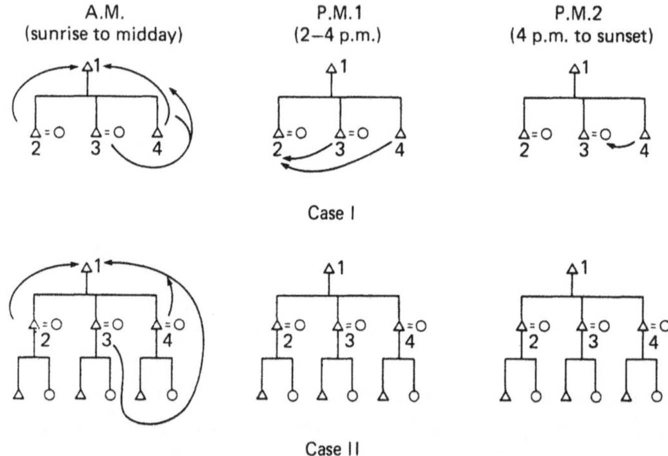

Fig. 2.2 The daily organization of farm labour among the Soninké, Mali. Case I: Paternal unit with married and unmarried juniors, no children. Case II: Paternal unit with married juniors and children: shift towards individuation.

Source: Pollet and Winter (1971).

expresses the fluidity and complexity of work arrangements.

The Soninké are primarily a patrilineal-based society and workgroups are built around paternal or fraternal domestic groups, with a hierarchy of juniors and seniors and associated dependency. A man's position in society is determined by who works for whom, and some men are not only givers or receivers of labour, but are both. Like Goody, Pollet and Winter are much concerned with the fission of groups and the formation of new workgroups based on a three-generational pattern, where either paternal or fraternal units are the norm. Their observations among the Soninké give some excellent detail of how farm work is organized, especially how the work done by juniors for seniors is varied

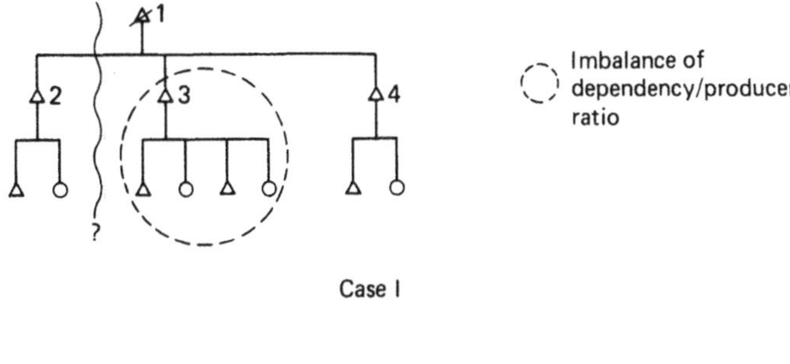

Case I

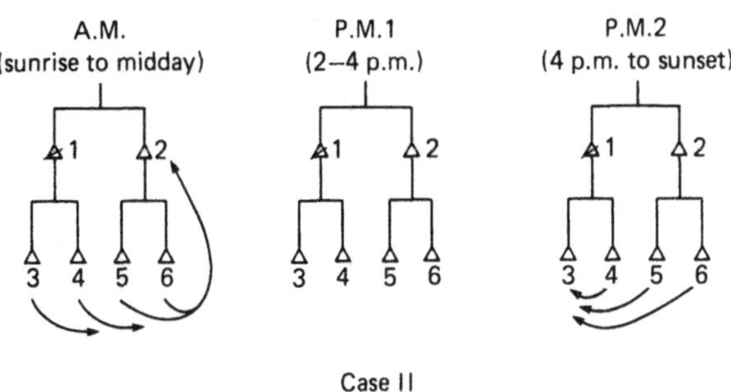

Case II

Fig. 2.3 The fission of domestic groups and the organization of farm labour among the Soninké, Mali. Case I: Father dies, and a fraternal unit is formed which may split at the wish of the senior brother if an imbalance develops. Otherwise, labour flows to senior brother in the same way as it formerly did to father. Case II: Death of senior brother, and fraternal unit continues briefly before fission takes place.

Source: Pollet and Winter (1971).

throughout the day and during the course of the week. What Pollet and Winter demonstrate is a whole plurality of workgroups within a hierarchical system, with groups forming, re-forming and dividing to achieve an equilibrium in terms of their constituent members. For our purpose, two important factors emerge: the size and composition of groups, and the labour flows among them; this can be best understood by looking at the sets of diagrams in Figures 2.2 and 2.3.

First, it is necessary to understand that the working day is organized into three periods: the morning session, usually from 7 a.m. to noon; followed by two afternoon sessions comprising 2 p.m. to 4 p.m. and 5 p.m. to 7 p.m. These periods are referred to in the diagrams as A.M. and P.M.1 and P.M.2. In the first diagram (2.2) we see a paternal unit which is the origin of all the other situations. Here three dependent sons work for the father in the morning, whereas in the afternoon he works alone while the senior brother receives work from his two juniors. In the final session the second brother receives work from the most junior. This situation is most likely if the sons are unmarried, or married with no, or few, children. On the other hand, if they have their own dependent children an alternative schedule is possible, where the brothers work for the father only in the morning; the remainder of the time they work on their own plots. On the fifth and sixth days (Thursdays and Fridays) special work arrangements obtain: no one works for the head and either there is a shift in favour of the eldest brother, or all work individually.

But what happens when the father dies? The paternal group then becomes a fraternally-based one whose members may continue to farm together, or as time passes and imbalances develop it may split into two or more domestic units. For example, in the situation described by Figure 2.3 the senior brother, on whom the others are dependent, has fewer children than his immediate junior, whose contribution to the unit's production may be less than he takes from it, in terms of consumption by himself and his growing number of dependants. Therefore the senior brother may decide that the groups should split, and it is he for whom everyone works a period of time who takes the decision to free his dependants. The decision may hinge on whether the children of his junior brothers are now old enough to help their fathers; also the split may be along lines of uterine filiation (that is, in polyganous societies) as the sons of different mothers may ultimately provide the patterns for fission within a fraternal group. But the decision of the senior brother to split the groups generally comes about when the labour of his dependants rather than producing a 'surplus' produces a 'loss' and his burden increases, so a split is made to achieve a better equilibrium based on optimum numbers.

As we noted earlier a whole plurality of groups is possible, but a few others are worth mentioning. In a fraternal group, if a junior dies his dependants will be absorbed by the senior member, but what if the reverse happens and it is the senior who dies first? If no split occurs then a restructuring with a double shift at the level of two generations takes place. In the morning the junior brother, now the head, requires labour from all his sons and his deceased brother's children, but in the second afternoon work period it is the eldest son of the deceased brother (formerly the head of the unit) who now receives labour from his cousins. This is one of the most fragile of work groups and according to Pollet and Winter rarely continues for more than a year or two, even if the situation among cousins remains unaltered by births and marriages. The exception is that a bachelor is never autonomous, therefore a man would work for his cousins, possibly only in the mornings, until he himself marries.

The outcome of these studies by Pollet and Winter on the social organization of labour indicates the varying size and composition of work groups, the fluctuation of labour flows throughout the day and week, as well as the effects of birth, death and marriage on labour relations. Work arrangements are also tied to land, and its allotment to members of a group; they also point out the difference between the large communal plot operated under the authority of the head and the smaller plots operated by subordinates. Plots are given according to the capacity to cultivate land and the product of the labour from these plots accrues to the individuals concerned. Obviously labour is shifted around the 'respective' farms and juniors may work on the head's farm, his elder brother's farm and his own plot in the course of a day or week. But when juniors reach working age they receive plots and may be provided with assistance to clear their land. Sometimes land is in a subsidiary village; then the family group is geographically split, and relations of dependency have to be modified either by gifts replacing labour, or by a son being sent to the head on Saturdays and Sundays.

Joint consumption unites men of different farming units and each man contributes grain for the benefit of the larger group. In most cases the senior provides millet and maize for the whole group on five days, while married juniors give their share on the two other days; thus the juniors contribute in a supplementary fashion to the group's subsistence. In some cases it may be customary to provide grain according to one's individual contribution to the group effort, but in reality increased contributions are often required if the need arises. In theory, obligations to provide are owed by the senior, or according to individual contribution, but in practice they may be owed indiscriminately by granaries which have food available. But it should be noted that, as with the Gouro, the complete process of production and distribution is combined into a single system regulated by redistribution organized by the senior member. The traditional role of the senior as the provider of food is historically linked to the pre-colonial period when slave labour was used, and granaries of the heads of segmentary, or kin-based, units were invariably full; since then adjustments have been made, and more flexible arrangements are required. Likewise, since the ending of slavery the large family labour groups have become subject to dislocation, and fission is common in order to ease the burden on the senior, who can no longer support so many dependants, given that extra-family labour in the form of slaves is no longer available.

SUMMARY

Age, sex and kin provide a basic framework for the organization of domestic groups, whose members are bound together by varying degrees of responsibility and dependence. Patterns of inheritance and property relations can also influence the nature and form of productive relations. The effectiveness of domestic groups as units of agricultural production requires a continuous redistribution of labour, either among their internal fractions or between them and movements of labour can be a vital part of the mobilization, allocation and control of farm labour. The redistribution of workers and the formation of work groups may take place within an established hierarchy of dependence, although group farming does not necessarily pre-empt individual farming, and the two may exist in parallel. Groups may form and re-form on a daily basis within a weekly cycle, or the redistribution of labour may be more permanent, such as when adoption takes place. But domestic groups also experience developmental cycles, which can be closely related to patterns of labour use, production and consumption.

More fundamental changes in the structure and organization of domestic groups have occurred as they have been drawn into commodity production, which has brought about changes in the division of labour and the growth of individualism. Domestic groups of the kind we have been discussing contain latent individualism, which is activated as they are penetrated by the market economy. The production of adequate food can in many instances be achieved without a total commitment of members for every hour of every day; time is available for personal farms or non-farm activity alongside the communal effort. Some domestic groups formerly had slaves who did a good deal of farm work, while in some societies women perform the majority of tasks. Unused labour may be available, which can be devoted to new crops and individual farming enterprises; the question is, whether it is a voluntary, or necessary process, and to what extent it begins to conflict with food staples when priorities occur over the timing of labour inputs.

It is to the penetration of the market economy that we now turn, using the profiles of the domestic groups discussed in this chapter as 'base-lines' from which we can judge the changes in farm labour. The development of market relations in tropical Africa was accelerated (although not always started) by European intervention in the nineteenth and early twentieth centuries; more recently it has been associated with the growth of urban markets and the political and economic priorities of the nation state. Throughout tropical Africa, changes in the external and internal economic forces have led to a turning outwards of domestic groups, and their integration into the larger market economy.

3

FARM LABOUR AND THE MARKET ECONOMY

From 1830 to 1930 African agriculture underwent a phenomenal expansion, due to the development of small-scale commercial farming, which radically changed many rural communities. Commercial farming existed prior to this period in some areas, for example in the Mandinka and Hausa-Fulani states of the western and central Sudan, but the expansion of existing crops and the introduction of new ones altered the scale and geographical distribution of commercial agriculture. Of particular importance were crops such as cocoa, cotton, coffee, groundnuts and oil palm, which were grown primarily for overseas markets. New patterns of cultivation were developed in association with the activities of European traders, the penetration of foreign merchant capital, the enterprise of indigenous farmers and traders and finally colonial rule. Tosh (1980) described it as a 'cash-crop revolution', a sentiment which is justified by the contribution of African agriculture to world trade, as well as the expansion of the market economy within Africa. The production of commercial crops for overseas markets continued after 1930 and today forms a source of income for many African farmers. But since 1930 the international commodity market has been unstable, despite efforts to check this by means of co-operatives and commodity agreements, and in many export countries export crops have shown a decline.

Although the development of export crops has been of such importance in changing African agriculture, one should not forget the parallel expansion of agricultural production for local markets, especially food staples to meet the burgeoning demand from groups of small-scale commodity producers and the increasing number of urban dwellers. In Central Africa peasant production of food for the settler labour market was important; in Northern Rhodesia by 1935 African farmers were producing almost half of the marketed maize in the territory, as production was stimulated by the development of copper mining. However, once this became a threat to the precariously-balanced European farming economy, future participation was curtailed by the introduction of quotas. In Southern Rhodesia during the 1960s, when European farmers became involved with tobacco production, once again it was the small-scale farmer who began to supply food staples to the industrial and urban areas.

In West Africa the increased incomes of small farmers engaged in export crop production from the nineteenth century onwards raised the demand for local, as well as imported food, and there was a growing demand from the urban areas. Today around Africa's largest towns there is a periphery of intensive agriculture where production systems are geared to providing food for urban populations, with all the concomitant pressure on land and the increase in landless farm workers. This in effect represents another important revolution, albeit on a more geographically-restricted scale, which has occurred since the 1950s and has gathered momentum in many countries since Independence. The commercialization of tropical African agriculture and its effects on the organization of labour have been profound, but they have also taken place with remarkable speed. In some regions in a matter of fifty to a hundred years semi-subsistence communal cultivators have become small-scale commodity producers, economically linked to national and international markets; moreover their communities now contain numerous permanent or transient migrant workers. On the other hand there are regions of tropical Africa outside the coastal littorals, commercial crop zones, mining enclaves and urban areas, which have experienced only marginal changes in their patterns of agricultural organization; or they may have become suppliers of migrant labour, in which case agriculture also has undergone significant changes.

In areas where farmers are primarily interested in producing for market there is still a good deal of semi-subsistence production, often involving a seasonal alternation of food and cash crops. The co-existence of non-capitalist and capitalist relations of production has sparked-off numerous debates about the transformation of communal cultivators to peasant farmers and the paths of transition towards capitalist relations of production and the emergence of an agricultural proletariat. The themes of 'peasantization' and 'proletarization' occupy an increasing space in the literature of rural development and change in tropical Africa, together with discussions of differentiation within rural societies. Differentiation is about the growing penetration of market relations of production and whether there has occurred a process of differentiation of rural dwellers into a class of capitalist farmers on the one hand, and a poorer class of agricultural labourers on the other hand, with an intermediate class of self-sufficient household producers, who are gradually 'squeezed out' as differentiation proceeds.

An alternative analysis looks at the growth of commodity production and considers how a distinctive peasant economy made up of small household producers has survived with a remarkable degree of control over family labour and land. Some of those who have adopted this line of argument will concede that differences do exist within peasantries; but not only do farmers keep some control over their land and labour, but they are also able to resist changes stemming from both market forces and State intervention. Furthermore, conflicts do not arise in rural societies because of internal class differences, but out of contradictions between peasants and the State (Williams, 1982). Household producers are also successful in providing commodities more cheaply than either capitalist or state agricultural complexes and paradoxically it is in the interests of the capitalist sector to encourage and maintain peasant producers. Finally, there is much in the nature of farming, such as high-risk, perishable produce and a protracted return on capital, which contributes to the survival of the peasant producers.

Harris (1982) believes that both perspectives – 'differentiation' and 'the peasant economy' – are useful and not mutually exclusive. This seems a reasonable assumption and furthermore it seems appropriate to look at both arguments as possible models which apply differentially over space and time. The differentiation argument looks more convincing in the agricultural peripheries of large towns and in the later stages of the development of commercial cropping. A case for considering the differential impact of market relations over space and time is made by Cliffe (1977) in the context of East Africa, based upon local circumstances and variations in colonial policy. He suggests four categories: (1) labour-supply areas; (2) cash-crop-producing areas; (3) quiescent areas; and (4) frontier areas. The first two are familiar categories; 'quiescent' refers to those areas where non-capitalist forms of production were little disturbed, and 'frontier zones' are those into which African populations expanded and where new patterns of production emerged, generally of a capitalist nature. It is however necessary to point out that there are both neo-classical and Marxian analyses of African production which believe that the term peasant is inappropriate, at least in the sense of using it as a separate economic category rather than a general descriptive term, and we shall return to this issue later, after briefly looking at some of the characteristics of African peasantries.

AFRICAN PEASANTS AND SMALL-COMMODITY PRODUCTION

Klein (1980) observes that defining peasants and producing typologies can be a barren exercise, especially if it obscures processes of change and creates a static picture of the rural sector. Yet when looking at social and economic changes one cannot avoid asking 'a change from what to what'? One answer to this question is that domestic production and consumption founded largely on age, sex and kinship have been turned outwards, and made increasingly dependent on external structures and market forces. But what is the dynamic that moves individuals and communities along this axis of change towards new productive relationships? Some writers have found this to lie in the transfer of surpluses to dominant groups or rulers, who underwrite their own standard of living and distribute remuneration to non-farmers in return for goods and services. In other words there is a general concept of 'rent' in the form of surplus produce passing upward from peasants who are at a lower level in a class hierarchy.

Post (1972) believes that state formation marks the threshold of transition between food cultivators in general, and peasants in particular, where there are power holders outside the cultivators' own social structures. He suggests two models, onc of communal producers, the other of peasant producers and he examines their inherent characteristics and transition from one to the other, and their incorporation into world capitalist networks. Communal cultivators are approximately equivalent to a mode of production based on communal land ownership, social division of labour based on kinship, where markets are absent or peripheral, and a political hierarchy largely co-terminous with kinship and cultural homogeneity. Alternatively, the peasant condition comprises individual ownership of land, a separation between the social division of labour and that vested in kinship, the presence of a market principle and separation of a political hierarchy and kinship, and finally the opposition of great and little cultures.

The relationship between the producer and the land raises the difficult issue of land tenure and the widespread occurrence of usufruct in tropical Africa. In European peasantries, property rights in land and goods were the basis for the formation of social groups and interpersonal relations either of a contractual or temporary kind. Land ownership was either by the peasant himself, or by the landlord who rented land to peasants, or who allowed them to share-crop land with no guarantee of tenure. In Africa the ascribed and indestructible membership of a kinship group can determine property rights, and social relationship and ownership of land is mediated through the communal groups. Communal possession does not necessarily imply communal use of land or communal organization of production. Communal possession and distribution is about how members (families or individuals) gain access to land and who are the socially-defined organizers of production; about how access is achieved and how it is defined and regulated under conditions of communal allocation (Clarke, 1980). Also there is no general sense in which possession of land is incompatible with the production and sale of commodities for one or more markets. The production of foods and cash crops can be (and is) carried out within the context of communal possession and control of access by the community.

It can be argued that what becomes important is whether or not the product of a man's labour becomes his private property, and that with the development of cash crops there is a tendency to use the land as if it belonged to individuals to a point where community ownership can be superseded, yet land is still not a marketable commodity. In Africa the use of land and property rights are not identical, and it is where property rights determine the control the producer has over the fruits of his labours that they become of paramount importance. In the pre-colonial Hausa-Fulani states, forms of ownership were important since land was given to classes of warriors and officials, who gave it out to others and collected taxes and used large slave populations to work farmland.

'Peasantization' is usually held to involve a movement towards the market principle, where the market process begins to structure the allocation of resources, income and outputs. Thus farmers become incorporated into wider exchange patterns, currency becomes a universal medium of exchange, speculation occurs and merchant capital becomes established. Another condition for an emerging peasantry is the role of the State: the State is a political hierarchy based on territory rather than kinship, and where obligations are enforced by power rather than mutually-recognized kinship duties. The development of such economic and political conditions in Africa has been associated with the penetration of European merchant capital, and unequal terms of exchange, all of which were eventually underwritten by colonial rule. But 'peasantization' also occurred in pre-colonial Africa, notably in the Sudanic states of West Africa, which were remarkable for their urbanism, systems of taxation, social division of labour and trading networks. Colonialism greatly encouraged the market principle and either new states were imposed where none had existed before, or indigenous ones were modified outside Africa on a much larger scale than had been known previously.

For many social scientists and some African historians the central attribute of a peasantry is contact with the international capitalist system, and peasants can be distinguished from subsistence cultivators by their involvement in the market and submission to other social classes. But such definitions and analyses are less clear-cut when they are applied to specific instances, both historical and contemporary. The dividing line between subsistence cultivator and peasant is often fuzzy, indeterminate and susceptible to change. Within a community there may exist differing degrees of commitment, or reliance on extenal markets where individual production units may shift towards either end of a spectrum that encompasses both subsistence cultivator and small-scale capitalist farmer. A distinction has been made between peasants who rely entirely on family labour, and whose outputs only are commoditized, and small-commodity producers who rely on unpaid family labour as well as being dependent on the market for the sale of their surpluses and the source of their daily needs. Beyond the small-commodity producers lie the small rural capitalist farmers who are net hirers of labour. But again the issue is complicated by the fact that at certain times other farmers may hire-in labour to offset temporary labour shortages, which result from adverse dependency ratios in the domestic production unit caused by the developmental cycle and age–sex imbalances.

The production of agricultural produce for capitalist markets has led to considerable differentiation within villages and the emergence of poor and rich households. Indications of these differences and incipient class relations are to be found in the amount of hired labour used, the individuation of land-use leading to renting and purchase, and the general commoditization of farming inputs and outputs. For many observers it is not the category of producers (for example, peasants) which is important in rural societies, but the degree of differentiation among them and the form and process of differentiation which has its roots in the existence of commodities and the purchase of labour. Writers such as Ennew *et al.* (1977) have argued that 'peasant' as a theoretical term signifying a distinct economic category has no place in Marxist writings. 'Peasant' refers to either feudal or semi-feudal tenants, or to petty-commodity producers who, although they may comprise a class, are not a distinct economic category and do not form a peasant mode of production. According to Ennew, both Lenin and Kautsky believed that peasantries were a heterogeneous collection of groups and classes who existed as part of capitalist relations of production. In essence, small-commodity producers are linked to, and part of, capitalist commodity circulation without being *necessarily* capitalist entrepreneurs, and they may still rely to a large extent on family labour.

Non-Marxist writers have also expressed reservations about the term peasant used in a specific sense and, for example, Polly Hill sees the cocoa migrants and Hausa farmers among whom she worked as exhibiting a high degree of social and economic differentiation and puts her emphasis on small farmers as entrepreneurs or rural capitalists (Hill, 1970). Sara Berry (1975) believes that cocoa production in Ghana and western Nigeria created neither a peasantry nor a fully-fledged system of agricultural capitalism. Hopkins (1976) points out the danger of creating analytical categories to verify in Africa a sequence of events derived fom the history of other continents. He goes on to add that African agrarian production does not readily lend itself to classifications inspired by European and Latin-American studies; landlords are not widely recognizable as a class or group and other elements of the rural economy such as pastoralists are not encompassed by peasant analysis. On this last point it should be noted that animal rearing and herding is not necessarily distinct from sedentary agriculture, and many farmers keep animals while others have important symbiotic relationships with pastoralists.[1]

It is neither possible, nor appropriate to pursue the arguments further about 'peasantization' and the development or otherwise of capitalist relations of production, but in the light of the issues they raise we must look at the ways in which domestic groups have adapted and changed their organization and allocation of labour to meet market demands. On the one hand agrarian production units have experienced only marginal disturbance, while on the other they have experienced diminution, and changes in their internal division of labour as both food and non-food crops have been extended to produce cash incomes. In some cases larger domestic groups have been advantageously placed when they have introduced commercial crops into their cultivation systems, but there does seem to be a general decay of complex groups and a shift towards smaller conjugal groupings which provide the nuclei for residence and production. Even so, one has to be careful because simple production units have the ability to expand seasonally or daily to meet specific needs as they integrate non-resident kin, hired labour and communal labour; flexibility is very characteristic of African farming households. Also, produc-

[1] Rodney Hilton, writing of European peasantries, stresses the specific character of peasantries in different historical epochs. The peasants of France differed profoundly before and after the Revolution, and 'there is all the greater contrast between the peasantries of medieval Europe and the peasantries of the neo-colonial world under the political and economic pressures of the great powers and the international companies' (Hilton, 1975).

tion units may be relatively large for the organization of food production, while splitting up into simple units for the production of cash crops. Smaller overall farming households have also meant an alteration in the internal division of labour by age and sex, as well as a new division along the lines of food versus cash crops.

The amount of social and economic differentiation which has occurred within rural communities is of considerable importance in the use and organization of farm labour; as we observed earlier, some farmers have extended their farms and become specialist producers and net hirers of labour. For example, small capitalist farmers have emerged in south-eastern Ghana as shallot growers, while among the Buganda cotton and coffee have led to the commoditization of farm inputs and outputs. In addition to hiring labour by the hour or day, African farmers make use of share-cropping and shared-labour systems and there has been a general increase in the mobility of farm labour, as farmers have produced for the market. Migrant labour has become an adjunct to farming as relatively-scarce local supplies in one area have been supplemented by migrant workers; while in another domestic groups have sent members into areas where commercial cropping is more advanced, or into towns to earn money to supplement farm incomes. It is now increasingly difficult to look at farming as either a distinct or even a primary activity; non-farm work, either engaged in locally or further afield, is a vital element in total household incomes, or for specific purposes such as accumulating bridewealth. Thus the reproduction of the domestic group is rooted in complex and flexible production relationships, which are no longer contained either within a domestic group or the local community.

The introduction of commercial crops has created new demands on the farming household's labour, expressed in the hours worked and when, the timing of inputs, and the shortage of labour due to clashes between different crops and their labour requirements. Many new crops such as cotton, cocoa and groundnuts did not require technical innovation as part of their successful cultivation, but, given that they were grown by labour-intensive methods within environments with a marked seasonal rainfall, they did require adjustments in the organization of labour if they were to be grown, as well as food staples. In turn this meant either adjustment being made internally within domestic production units, or an increasing use of external labour inputs through hiring labour; in both cases productive relationships were altered. When considering the impact of agrarian change due to an increased involvement with local and international markets, it is appropriate that we begin (as we did in Chapter 1) by looking at the seasonal distribution of labour, and how this relates to cultivation practices, before we move on to look at internal re-arrangements of labour and the use of external sources.

THE SEASONAL DEPLOYMENT OF LABOUR AND THE MARKET ECONOMY

Among small farmers the successful cultivation of cash crops (at least in the first instance) is intimately related to integrating them into an established complex of food crops. Such integrated patterns of cultivation are a relevant issue in the context of the 'cash-crop revolution', as well as, today, in the context of attempts by the State to modernize agriculture, or farmers who are entering new urban markets. It is true that as long as the majority of farming groups uses labour-intensive methods, and either in whole, or in part, the reproduction of the labour force depends upon the production of food staples, then the successful allocation of labour between food and non-food crops is of paramount importance. But as we have seen in Chapter 1, the seasonal nature of farming and labour bottlenecks are major constraints on production, and there are also differences between forest and savannah environments, as well as the many micro-environments with which farmers have to cope.

It has been argued that the introduction of cash crops such as cotton and groundnuts into savannah regions presents greater difficulties than the introduction of cocoa, coffee, rubber and palm oil into the forests (Tosh, 1980). It is certainly true that the wet season is more limited in the savannahs, whereas in the forests the growing season is much longer and the labour peaks for tree crops and food staples exhibit some complementarity. But a great deal depends on the type of food crop grown; for example, in Ghana the combination of cocoa with plantains and cocoa-yams gives a good measure of complementarity, as the emphasis on food staples comes from February to June, while July to January is when the chief inputs on cocoa are needed (Beckett, cited in Cleave, 1974). However, when rice is grown there is a considerable clash between harvesting this crop and cocoa planting and weeding. Villages in Nigeria where yams and maize are grown have a rather better degree of integration, and better still when cassava is the main crop, as the labour inputs are smaller and regularly spaced throughout the year (Galletti, cited in Cleave, 1974). But in all cases cocoa generates the greatest seasonal fluctuation in labour demand, and the demand, and the extent to which seasonality can be modified appears to vary greatly with the complementarity of food and cash crops, with grains giving the least flexibility. Since cocoa was introduced there is evidence of a shift to those food staples which reduce clashes, and this is important for those farmers who cannot afford much hired labour.

The chief commercial crops grown in savannahs are cotton and groundnuts, which have to be cultivated with food crops such as sorghum, millets and maize in a growing season which may be as little as six months. Compared with forests, the shorter growing season in savannahs is an added problem when growing food and cash crops, and the degree of flexibility may be less, especially in the range of alternative food crops. Cotton is particularly demanding of labour and requires correctly-timed planting at regular intervals, periodic thinning, constant weeding and rapid and careful harvesting. Observations from Tanzania (Sukumuland) show that 600 man hours per acre are required for cotton compared with 380 for sorghum, and there is simultaneous competition for these inputs over a relatively limited growing season (Von Rotenhan, 1968).

An example of seasonal labour use from Uganda can be used to demonstrate the deployment of labour over the season and the problems farmers have in combining food staple with cotton (Fig. 3.1). In January and February rainfall is very low, but in March the 'rains' begin and land has to be prepared for millet while sweet potato mounds are dug and the land is made ready for cotton. By May the first weeding of millet is done and cotton has been planted, and last year's cassava is harvested to break the hungry season. But the peak labour demand is in July when cotton planting has to be finished, early millet harvested, groundnuts weeded, and sesame beds prepared. Cotton picking begins in December and runs on into January and although hours are long, work is lighter. Looking at the distribution of work throughout the year it might appear that there is a complementarity between the major food staple, millet, and the chief cash crop, cotton: the peak labour input for millet is in March-April when work on cotton is minimal. But this 'complementarity' is achieved through a re-organization of cropping to avoid conflicting labour demands. The planting of cotton is spread over May to July, which is not the way to get the best yields of cotton. Similar problems are encoun-

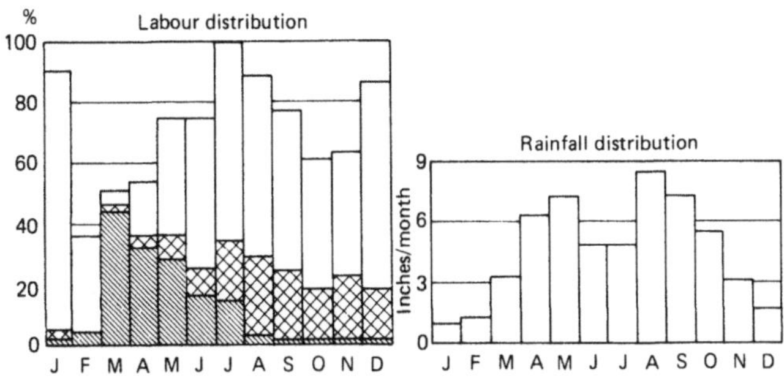

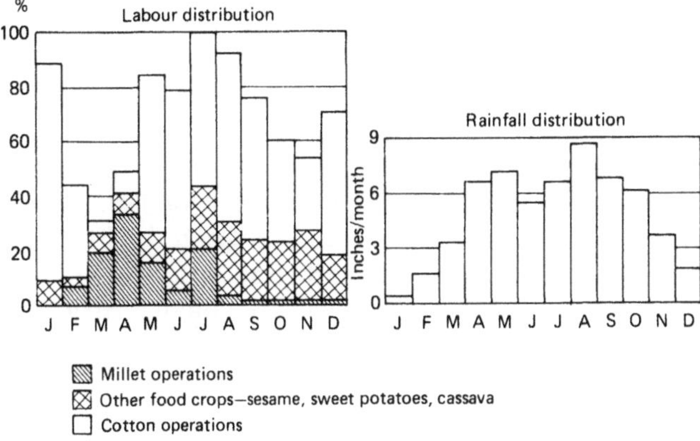

Fig. 3.1 The seasonal distribution of labour: cotton farms, northern Uganda, modified from histograms supplied by M. Hall, cited in Cleave (1974), p. 87.

tered in northern Nigeria, where the Cotton Board frequently complains that farmers leave the planting of cotton too late to get good yields; not surprisingly, farmers do this to secure their millet and guinea-corn crops. There are of course those farmers who have access to sufficient labour, or can hire it, and so treat both crops in the best manner possible, giving them better yields and ultimately higher incomes. Although the introduction of cash crops has been successfully incorporated into indigenous farming systems, it has not been done without adaptation and a certain amount of resistance, and has been accompanied by increased differentiation among domestic groups.

The shift towards cultivation systems which comprised cotton and groundnuts was brought about in several ways. First, by varying degrees of economic compulsion by the colonial powers and their successors; second, by prices being sufficiently attractive to make the effort worthwhile; third, by the increasing use of hired labour and the development of capitalist relations of production. There is no doubt that in some areas farmers were either resistant to certain crops, or preferred others according to the strength and relative importance of these different factors. Often the marketing of food crops was preferred as it reduced the difficulty of allocating labour between food staples and non-food staples; this was the case in Central Africa in the 1930s and 1960s. Also, the marketing of food staples has probably a much longer history in pre-colonial Africa than is generally accepted, or has indeed been investigated. The pre-colonial urban populations of West Africa and the specialist division of labour necessitated the supply of food to towns, and this may have been the case elsewhere in Africa. Commercial crops, such as groundnuts, were often successful, as they could be used as a food crop; this is partly why the Kano groundnut zone flourished (also sesame in Tivland) and during the 1914–18 famine a large proportion of the crop was eaten and not sold (Hogendorn, 1978). But, from the point of view of the colonial governments, food crops did not generate external trade, or supply the demands of the *métropoles*, and in some areas they successfully diverted farmers into export-crop production. From the turn of the century in Central Africa, the government intervened in the food market to protect the white interests supplying the settler market (Palmer and Parsons, 1977). In the Kano area they were less successful, as the intention was to produce cotton in this region, but local farmers, assisted by the entrepreneurial activities of local merchants and the credit they provided, turned this into a commercial groundnut zone, largely as a result of the better prices offered for groundnuts (Hogendorn, 1978).

Where the dominant cash crop did not serve as a food crop, and where the labour demands of crops such as cotton proved disruptive of farming schedules, there is considerable evidence of farmers growing alternative food crops or increasing the output of what had formerly been subsidiary crops. Cassava has undergone a remarkable expansion and diffusion in the past fifty years and part of its present prominence as a food crop is due to its adaptability to a wide range of soil and rainfall conditions and particularly the low labour inputs it requires. Also it can be left or stored in the ground from one season to another and used as an insurance against main-crop failure, or shortages arising from poor weather or insufficient labour. After the compulsory introduction of cotton production in Ogbangui in 1926 cassava production was rapidly expanded; similarly in the Oriental Province of the former Belgian Congo and the Zande district of Sudan (Jones, 1959). It has been estimated that some 48 per cent of the crop area of tropical Africa now contains some cassava. But the shift towards new food and non-food crops has involved changing the internal division of labour in many production units, so that women have become the principal suppliers of food in rural households.

WOMEN AND THE DEVELOPMENT OF COMMERCIAL FARMING

The sexual division of labour within farming groups can be materially altered by the introduction of new crops as the demand for labour rises in general, or at particular points in the cultivation cycle. Also, patterns of marriage and reproduction may be influenced by new farming practices, together with the opportunities for non-farm work which become available primarily for men. It is important therefore to look at how the re-allocation of male and female labour occurs within farming groups as they become producers for local and international markets.

An interesting case of the impact of commercialization on traditional farming is contained in some work done by Guyer (1980) on cocoa farming among the Beti of southern Cameroon. Guyer makes the general point that changing patterns of food production have been explained on the one hand by population pressure on land, and on the other by the penetration of the market principle and the differential prices of crops. She suggests that the management of both these constraints depends on the rather broader social and economic contexts in which decisions are made. Boserup (1970) and Meillasoux (1981) have pointed out that the social position of women farmers differs from men at the local level, and economically at the regional and national levels, as they work under different constraints, and have differing opportunities for alternative employment. As men have become more involved with commercial crops they have correspondingly had more access to consumer goods, which has also been the case when men have taken up non-farm work; these changes in men's work have had an independent effect on cropping patterns, frequently requiring an internal adjustment of the sexual division of labour within farming groups.

The traditional cultivation systems of the Beti rest on a two-field rotational bush-fallow system: a large field (*esep*) cleared in the forest by men and planted with melon seeds and yams, with subsidiary crops of taro and plantain; a smaller field, or intensively-cultivated plot (*afub awondo*) farmed by women and planted chiefly with groundnuts. Guyer argues that cocoa growing has increased income-dependency on cocoa markets, altered population–land ratios of food crops, and increased the dependence for food staples on the elaboration of women's smaller plots (*afub awondo*), with a corresponding decline in yam production. These changes have been brought about by the re-allocation of male labour towards the cocoa economy while women have sustained traditional patterns of cultivation (albeit modified) because of the absence of alternative opportunities for them either in new crops or new jobs. After the withdrawal of male labour from porterage in the 1920s, male labour was diverted into cocoa farming which became exclusively men's work. Cocoa fitted men's traditional agricultural expertise in bush-farming and was the means of tax-payments.

Although the total labour demand of cocoa was small, the harvest period coincided with the November harvest of yams and melon seeds and this led to the partial substitution of cocoa for these food crops. Hitherto melon seeds had an exchange value against iron-bar currency, but eventually cocoa became equivalent to melon seeds when indigenous currency was outlawed in 1925. The former tension between elders and young men wishing to accumulate melon seeds as a source of wealth was replaced by cocoa farms. Until the abolition of the *indigénat*[1] in 1946, cocoa farming was in the hands of big-men farmers using village labour, but after this date there was a surge of individualization among men and a collapse in traditional political authority, as mothers and wives became the providers of food staples and responsible for the immediate reproduction of the household. It also became more difficult to assemble large

[1] The *indigénat* was a disciplinary code used by French administrators who, under its terms, could impose arbitrary penalties on African 'non-citizens'. In particular, it was used to sanction forced labour and to prohibit personal mobility.

groups of men to clear the traditional large yam farm, and farming households decreased in size as extended complex units declined. In the 1950s the average farming household had no more than five members, with two or three active adults; sex ratios and marriage patterns changed and in the 1970s the ratio of male to females was 100:130, due to out-migration. And of those females aged sixteen years and above only 56 per cent were married.

The old division of labour associated with the rights and duties of marriage was no longer the basis of production, especially for the growing proportion of women without husbands. Male labour was less available because of cocoa and out-migration, yet until the 1960s women had little alternative employment either in food processing or trading because of the lack of local commercialized food markets. However, in the 1970s there were some signs of women re-allocating their labour in response to the price incentives of local markets for foodstuffs. But generally women were providing the means of subsistence and reproduction of farming units based on nuclear, or joint-families, while men were using cocoa income for luxuries and tax-payments. The result was the increased use of individual female farming plots (*afub awondo*): by 1959 the fields contained 80 per cent cassava, 39 per cent groundnuts, while melon seeds were found in only 8 per cent of fields and yams in 28 per cent. We may note once again the shift towards cassava with its lighter labour demands and tolerance of a wide variety of soil conditions.

The large forest fields (*esep*) were still cultivated in the 1970s, but less intensively, and had become more dependent on their integration into women's farming schedules and whether male labour could be mobilized for clearing. The individual and female cycle of traditional farming has become the basis of food production, but women's fields are now larger than they were in the past, and more intensively interplanted, and women work longer hours. While Guyer (1980) stresses the importance of the social and economic organization of production as initiating change in land-use, she also points out that increased population has shortened fallows, which again gives a push away from the use of large forest fields, which require long periods of resting.

The growth of urban demand for food in southern Cameroon has begun to offer women a way of making a regular cash income, and men an alternative to cocoa farming. Production of both cocoa and food staples are integrated into a market system, and food farming has begun to reflect market prices. According to Guyer, the effect of these changes on cropping patterns will depend on the ways in which men and women, independently, and in joint-enterprise, will re-interpret the sexual division of labour and rights in each other's resources. The proximity of urban markets is a powerful influence on farming patterns and labour allocation in many parts of Africa; for example, by 1951, in the highly urbanized parts of south-west Nigeria, only 32 per cent of food consumed was home-grown, as much of the food produced was sold in local markets.

Changing patterns of food production and labour allocation in response to cash crops is paralleled in other parts of Africa and one particularly well-documented case is that of the Gambia, through the work of Haswell (1953, 1963) and later Weil (1973) and Dey (1980). In the Gambia there has been a reduction in millet and sorghum, the traditional food staples, cultivated by males, and an increase in the production of swampland rice by women. This adaptation to the increased penetration of the market has depended on competition for two basic resources: tidal swamp and skilled female labour. The partial commercialization of agriculture has largely been the product of the increased cultivation of groundnuts on dry upland farms, which has reduced the amount of sorghum and millet grown. Farmers have become small-commodity producers who buy in the greater proportion of their food, usually Burmesé imported rice, or they have developed alternative food sources within the household as women become responsible for basic foodstuffs.

Rice was traditionally a minor crop cultivated by women in rain-fed swamps, or depressions formed by small feeder streams of the River Gambia and there was no competition for resources between this system and upland systems of farming. But since the 1950s upland farms have increased the proportion of groundnut to food crops, which together with an extension of the cultivable area has led to shortages of labour. This situation has been exacerbated as patrilineal joint-families have given way to conjugal or nuclear ones as the basis for production and consumption. One result of this has been that internal labour resources of smaller units are less flexible and require a more efficient use of labour if to avoid hiring extra workers. Consequently there has been an intensive application of female labour to rain-fed rice swamps and where possible the development of tidal swamps. According to Weil (1973) in 1940 all Mandinka rice was grown in rain-fed swamps and the 80 per cent increase in rice production achieved between then and 1960 was largely due to the extension of rice cultivation into tidal swamps, where yields can be between two and four times greater. Swamp-rice cultivation has attracted many Mandinka villages towards the river banks in the quest for rice-land and skilled female labour.

Rights to swampland are vested in those who clear the swamp or inherit land through patrilineages which exercise stewardship over the use of land. Land cannot be sold, but it is loaned , which spreads risks and can be a source of power and clientage. Those who first inhabited the riverine areas hold the most accessible land, while later arrivals have had to gain access through kinship or by developing affinal relationships. In a recently-established village studied by Weil, three-quarters of the rice plots were rain-fed and of these 84 per cent were borrowed, with about half from non-relatives. In the case of the swampland rice farms, 93 per cent were borrowed. Loans of land came from villages with whom there were strong historical ties and where marriages had been made to gain access to resources. But the relationships were clearly asymmetric; Weil's sample village was taking more women from the land-rich ones than they sent. This led to an increase in exogamous marriages as new villages sought not only land but women who were skilled in swamp-rice farming. Marriage ties and land-loaning have become integrated, while those who have land to loan have increased their power base in local politics, often to the extent that they can influence the allocation of local development funds. Swampland cultivation in the Gambia reiterates the importance of marriage and marriage deals in the production and reproduction of domestic groups, as well as showing a trend away from patrilineal descent as the means whereby resources are secured, towards the establishment of affinal ties.

Haswell's work in another Gambian village, spanning the period 1950–60, has also shown the changing role of women as farmers. As the size of production units shrank and population remained relatively stable within the village, women began to enter adult production at an earlier age and to leave it later. Women now have lengthening careers associated with the shift to rice production in an economy where the cost of replacing or substituting food by imported rice is very costly; thus the roles and place of women in Mandinka society have changed. The production of groundnuts for market has been achieved indirectly through women working longer on subsistence crops, which has increased their independence and the amount of bridewealth demanded for those women skilled in swamp-rice farming. Also, divorce rates are up in the 25–35 years' age group, where women's rice farming potential is at its greatest (Haswell, 1953; 1963).

Reports of changes in the division of labour and the roles of women come from many parts of tropical Africa, and we may conclude this section with one more instance from Kenya. In East and Central Africa the presence of Europeans as settler-farmers and the development of industry and mining helped to curtail commercial farming by Africans in favour of labour recruitment, which frequently disrupted traditional production relations.[1] In the pre-colonial economy of Kenya the economic spheres of men and women were autonomous and complementary; land was vested in the patriclan and men assisted in cultivation while women exercised 'ownership' of the crops. In the colonial period, land was alienated and concepts of individual ownership were introduced which have been re-inforced since Independence. In many places in Western Kenya there is a well-developed land market and increasing landlessness, as richer peasants, school teachers, government officials and shopkeepers acquire land by purchase. The registration of land and the division of clan land into private plots has been to the advantage of men, with the position of women becoming more precarious. Also, men have become primarily interested in cash crops and non-farm employment, with women providing increasing amounts of labour for both subsistence and cash crops (Smock, 1981; Mönsted, 1977). Policies of colonial taxation and labour recruitment drew men into the non-farm sector, and many of them have become seasonal or permanent town dwellers. The result is that the position of men has become marginalized in the

[1] The situation was particularly bad in Central Africa, for example in the Belgian Congo and French Equatorial Africa where the Concessionary Company system was pronounced, together with forced labour, conscription and labour recruitment (see Birmingham and Martin, 1983).

context of farm work. When out-migration of men reaches levels which make traditional farm work difficult, households rely on remittances or marketable crops to get the cash needed to buy-in foodstuffs.

Kongstad and Mönsted (1980) examined the reproduction of labour and means of production among Kenyan peasant households and concluded that 60 per cent by value accrued from purchases, that is, additional food, other items of consumption, seed, machine-hiring, fertilizers, animal feed and wages. The remaining 40 per cent was domestically produced and included food seeds and animal feed. Kongstad and Mönsted's work was based on the Integrated Rural Survey and their own data, and they estimated that half the food consumed, by value, came from purchases and that some 29 per cent of males in rural areas were in wage employment. The implications are that men are becoming detached from the household economy in some rural areas, at least in terms of the manpower they supply for farming, especially for foodstuffs. Table 3.1 shows the relative commitment of household members to farm work in Nyanza, Western, and Rift Valley Provinces; the smaller proportion of men involved in working the land is quite striking, with even less participation by men in prosperous peasant households, who have now become 'farm-managers'. Women are now primarily responsible for foodstuff production, the purchase of foods and other items, and in this context their role as market traders is of some importance. Food production and trading is part of the circuit of subsistence and reproduction of households, and it is arguable that women have become exploited by men, as they appropriate their surplus labour. The data examined by Kongstad and Mönsted point to the fact that the productive efforts and trading of women is aimed at family reproduction, and not capital accumulation, although there are discernible differences between the average and the rich peasant household:

Table 3.1 *Who works on the land in Nyanza, Western and Rift Valley Provinces, Kenya?*

Percentage of household labour working in agriculture:	Peasant	Prosperous peasant
Wife	93	84
Husband	61	26
Children	87	86
Relatives	17	15
Percentage of households using non-domestic labour:		
Hired labour	39	87
Work groups	4	1
No information	1	nil

Source: Kongstad and Mönsted (1980).

the latter used more money to expand their trading. Kongstad and Mönsted emphasize the decline of the extended family in favour of nuclear families and they go further than this: because of the detachment of many men from their households, they tentatively suggest that a division of families has occurred into male and female spheres of production and reproduction.

THE CHANGING STRUCTURE OF DOMESTIC PRODUCTION

The introduction of new commercial crops and the increase in non-farm employment have been influential in eroding production relations based on extended kinship groups, leading to a radical alteration of the size and composition of domestic groups. The demise of large complex units and their replacement in whole or part by simpler conjugal-based groups is a crucial issue in the organization of farm labour, which is part of the crisis facing many agricultural producers in Africa at the present time. Therefore it is important to look at the causes of the emergence of smaller farming households and how they are reproduced. This issue forms a backward link with the previous discussion, in Chapter 2, of a domestic economy built on principles of age, sex and kin, as well as being an important element in the present discussion of commodity production and differentiation, and a forward link to the use of hired labour and the development of labour mobility. Let us look then at some further examples of changing domestic structures, and the effects and implications for the supply and organization of farm labour.

Agrarian households among the Hausa-Fulani in northern Nigeria have attracted the attention of several researchers who have been interested in the nature of and structure of agricultural production and the changes which have occurred over the past fifty years (Buntjer, 1973; Goddard, 1973; Hill, 1972, 1977; Norman, 1972; Goddard *et al.*, 1971; Shenton and Lennihan, 1981; Smith, 1955; Wallace, 1979). The household production unit (*gandu*; pl. *gandaye*) is ideally any combination of a senior male (*mai gida*) with his married and unmarried sons and brothers, and their sons and clients, wives and children, who comprise a joint consumption–production unit. This household form has much in common with those of the Mandinka described in Chapter 2, and similarly *gandaye* can be arranged around paternal or fraternal relationships. Like the Mandinka, work was traditionally organized communally on three days for the cultivation of crops grown for subsistence and taxes, while on the remaining days adult males worked on their own farms.

Working arrangements and eating arrangements are

fluid and consumption and production units are not necessarily co-terminous. The important attribute of the *gandu* is that the head has sets of obligations and responsibilities which are matched by the subordinates; traditionally the head organizes land, tools, and payment of taxes, arranges marriages and naming-ceremonies and represents the household in the village community. Although internal arrangements for work and consumption are varied, the head is responsible for the reproduction of the household and its continuance. One advantage of such extended units is that they comprise several nuclear families who are at different points in their life-cycles, and when they experience adverse dependency ratios (producers related to consumers) the larger household acts as a buffer and labour can be internally redistributed. The roots of *gandu* lie in precolonial society, when many domestic groups were much larger as they included slaves who added considerably to the labour force at the disposal of the *mai gida*.

Even if we discount both the effect of the development cycle on domestic groups and that men in their lifetimes may experience different types of household organization, there seems to be a good deal of evidence for the decline in the three-generational type of domestic grouping based on the close kinship of adult males. There is some consensus among several authors that now about one in five production units are based on fathers who have at least one dependent son who works with him, and about one in ten where brothers co-operate at least for a limited period, although it rarely survives the marriage of one of them. Wallace (1979) stresses that the nature of co-operation between men is very varied; sometimes it lasts just for the wet season; sometimes for a few days, and while most unmarried sons will work for their fathers it may be for a limited number of hours (for example, at week-ends) as their time is constrained by their other work as craftworkers, traders or wage labourers. It would appear that what is happening is that the old split-time system of three days on communal farms, and four on one's own has shifted so that the emphasis is now either on one's own farms related to a conjugal household, or to some non-farm job; the communal element of working with fathers and brothers has become vestigial, although it may strengthen in times of crises or need. We have, then, the skeletal remains of the *gandu* system, with kin still loosely connected in productive tasks and the facility remains to 'call' kin-based labour at particular times and to give security to aged parents as they become infirm. But the underpinnings of mutual responsibility have gone, and Goddard (1973) has proposed that there are three types of *gandu*: the traditional type, where the head is controlling a composite unit of production and reproduction; a modified type where each man pays his own taxes; and a third type, where conjugal production units have individual farms and responsibility for taxes and marriage dues, but they co-reside in a compound organized by a senior male who acts rather in the capacity of farm manager and intermediary between the compound and the village. In 1979 local community taxes were abolished, which further undermined the system. It can legitimately be asked whether such arrangements merit the term *gandu*, especially as labour is frequently hired by individual farming units within the compound.

Shenton and Lennihan (1981) give a graphic account of the processes of change within *gandaye* in northern Nigeria as the pre-colonial cotton industry was re-organized and expanded by the British in the early twentieth century. The British Cotton Growers' Association were given monopoly buying rights in 1905, and the company used agents as buyers, paying them commission. Competition among buyers led to the use of a cash-advance system for farmers, who responded to this incentive because they needed increased amounts of cash to take advantage of the increased availability of local and imported consumer goods, and the payment of taxes in British coinage. Perhaps more importantly, cash payments affected the cycle of social reproduction , as bridewealth became a transaction needing not just calabashes, local cloth and grain, but such things as enamel pots and sums of cash.

During the 1920s and 1930s a series of events led to greater socio-economic differentiation in the cotton-growing areas, which began to affect the structure of *gandaye*. Cotton prices were depressed in this period, famine occurred in 1926–7, and many families who had used their cash advances for bridewealth, weddings and naming-ceremonies were caught in a web of indebtedness and sold grain on a larger scale than hitherto. Those households that weathered these storms used their cash-advances to hire labour to expand their farms and were able to draw on an expanded labour pool comprising those who were in less fortunate circumstances. Thus the market for food and hired labour prospered. The situation for poorer farmers was exacerbated as they hired themselves out to wealthier farmers, and their own crops accordingly were dealt with at a later, and less propitious, point in the cultivation cycle. In this way Shenton and Lennihan believe differentiation proceeded in the cotton-growing areas. In some areas, notably the Kano region, farmers and local merchants resisted the introduction of cotton and preferred, and succeeded in growing, groundnuts, which yielded better prices and unlike cotton could be consumed in times of crisis (Hogendorn, 1978).

Shenton and Lennihan describe how the development of cotton growing affected not only the level of economic well-being among *gandaye* but brought about changes in their internal structure. Although it may be difficult to measure the decline in size of *gandaye* it is possible to chart the changing obligations and rights of members, which began to erode such farming households. Heads of *gandaye* provided tools, marriage expenses, personal plots of land, and paid taxes. Subordinates provided labour on communal farms, but kept the produce of their own plots and whatever they earned from non-farm work, which was especially important in the dry season. Under the conditions brought about by cotton farming and cash-advance systems, there emerged a group of heads who could no longer meet their obligations and accordingly reduced them. Taxes were paid from private plots, or from non-farm jobs; therefore the *gandu* was decentralized, and while the men might be grouped together for the purposes of organizing farming, the patterns of distribution and consumption were individualized.

Under these conditions the extended household system was weakened and the conjugal or nuclear family became the focus of production and consumption. In northern Nigeria, as in other parts of Africa, the process of change and decay of extended production units was also affected by the decline and abolition of domestic slavery under colonial rule. Many slaves left their former owners to set up their own farming households, while those who remained as clients enjoyed the opportunity of dry-season migration jobs formerly circumscribed by their status (Swindell, 1984). Also, labour migration became the means of greater access to goods from outside the local community, which could be used independently to finance marriages and naming-ceremonies as part of the cycle of reproduction.

In south-western Nigeria in the nineteenth century, large households with numerous slaves were engaged in the production of palm-oil and foodstuffs for local markets. However, such households were undermined as the colonial authorities created politico-legal institutions which have allowed the inheritance of land, its sale and the abolition of slavery (Clarke, 1981). The exit of slaves led to a decline in manpower and the fragmentation of households, which hitherto also had the benefit of slave-wives who were acquired without the need for bridewealth. A major condition of male independence was wives, but marriage was controlled by heads who themselves accumulated many wives. Once men were able to generate resources for marriage for themselves then households began to break up. The independence of junior males was encouraged by the cultivation of cocoa as a commercial crop on new bush farms in place of palm-oil; and there was little point in men cultivating cocoa farms for their fathers to accumulate more wives, when they could grow the crop themselves and ensure the reproduction of smaller households over which they had control. In turn, the breakdown of larger groups contributed to changes in the organization of farm labour; no longer were negotiations between fathers and sons, but between husbands and wives, together with the hiring-in of migrant workers as the need arose.

It is frequently argued that the decline in food production in Africa stems from the production of export crops required first by the colonial government, and now by independent governments needing foreign exchange. An alternative view is given by Isaacs (1982) who has studied rice farmers in Sierra Leone. His argument is that the decline in rice production is due to the changing size and composition of agrarian households, which is the result not simply of new export crops, but of the general monetization and commercialization of the economy over the past forty years. The Mende who inhabit the southern parts of Sierra Leone have households which are short of labour for rice production and have moved into cocoa and coffee farming to compensate for this. Table 3.2 shows part of an analysis made by Isaacs of household types, and although it is admittedly cross-sectional and fails to capture the dynamics

Table 3.2. *Household types and composition in Bambara Chiefdom, Sierra Leone*

Household type	Type as per cent of total households	Average number of adults	Average number of children
I. *Conjugal households*			
A. Monogamous households (non-extended)	41.7	3.0	1.6
B. Polyganous households (non-extended)	26.7	5.3	2.4
C. Lineally-extended households	0.0	0.0	0.0
D. Collaterally-extended households	13.3	5.9	2.8
E. Other consanguineally-extended households	3.3	9.0	4.5
F. Non-consanguineally-extended households	8.3	6.0	2.6
II. *Non-conjugal households*	6.6	1.2	0.0
	100.0		

Source: Isaacs (1982).

of the family life-cycle, it is useful for a comparison of extended and non-extended households at a point in time. It can be seen that household types A and B (monogamous non-extended and polyganous non-extended) account for 68.4 per cent of the total, and show the demise of the three-generational households.

The cultivation of upland rice farms in Mendeland requires that a man has at least four wives (Little, 1967), but only 25 per cent had enough women in 1967 at the time of

Isaacs' survey. Women are important for weeding and harvesting, while men prepare the fields and it takes about six men to control the burning of one acre of upland bush; in the survey, no household had more than five men. Children's work is quite important too, and they assist with harrowing and are responsible for bird scaring, but 18 per cent of households had no resident children and 26 per cent had only one. This kind of household structure was observed by Little in the urban and semi-urban areas in the 1940s, and now seems to have spread into the more rural areas. Thus the amount of rice grown is restricted by the availability of labour. On the one hand the reduction of male labour reduces the effectiveness or marginal utility of additional wives, while on the other male labour is only useful if complemented by female labour. The decline in the Mende farming household is explained by Isaacs as due to the monetization of the economy and the independence of young men as bridewealth became payable in cash, which in turn stimulated non-farm work. Income from non-farm work led to earlier fission, and after 1926 domestic slavery was abolished, which added to the problems of organizing and maintaining large farming households. From the 1930s onwards, the mining industry in Sierra Leone began to offer additional employment for men and by the 1950s the diamond-mining boom was well under way; this offered seasonal and longer-term non-farm employment for men as labourers and licensed small-scale diggers, as well as workers in the two large company mines.

The reduction in household sizes seems to be widespread and a continuing process in many parts of Africa and O'Leary (1983) has looked at the impact of population growth and labour migration on households in the Kitui region of the Eastern Province of Kenya; his account presents yet another gloss on this issue. Since the 1930s there has been population growth, drought and loss of cattle among the Kitui, who are an agro-pastoral group, and this has led to increased labour migration. But Kitui migrants re-invested earnings in the education of their children, a much-encouraged activity after Independence, and they have succeeded in getting their children better jobs, as well as investing in trade and livestock. Migration has in this instance been a source of quite specific economic and social differentiation among the Kitui. But among the Kitui several factors influence household sizes. Among brothers whose father has died, and who derive a large proportion of their incomes from migration, wives are placed in a common household and the women-folk continue to organize farming jointly. Also, in high-population density regions households tend to stay large, as they are less able to split because of the scarcity of land. O'Leary draws a contrast between high- and low-population density areas; in the former, household sizes average eleven adults, with about 60 per cent of the men aged between 21 and 62 years involved in off-farm work; in the latter, the average household size is nine, with only 30 per cent in non-farm work. But it appears that the wealth of households may or may not affect their size. Some rich men like large households as a matter of prestige, while others who may see themselves as 'new men' like to try and raise the living standards of their conjugal households. The question whether extended households tend to persist among the wealthier has been raised in other contexts (for example, Hill, 1972), but it seems uncertain whether this is the case; the members of the poorer household may have to stick together if they are to survive, but on the other hand they are the ones who feel the pressures of indebtedness and also lack resources, which encourages them to take up wage labour. Probably much depends on local conditions and whether there is land available or, if it is scarce, whether it has yet become a saleable commodity.

SUMMARY

The penetration of the market economy has profoundly altered rural communities in tropical Africa, although changes in agricultural production have not been evenly spread over time and space. In many rural areas now, the reproduction of domestic groups does not take place within localized networks of production and redistribution, but within larger social and economic spheres conditioned by the market for goods and labour. Production for the market may exacerbate seasonal labour bottlenecks, especially if both cash and subsistence crops are grown, and this may alter the division of labour between men and women. The involvement of men on non-farm and off-farm employment together with greater individualization of patterns of production and consumption have led to the decay of larger extended domestic groups, and there is a good deal of economic differentiation within rural communities.

But the development of commercial farming has not been achieved by domestic labour forces alone; the hiring of local labour or long-distance migrant workers has been and continues to be a striking feature of crop production for internal use, as well as for export. Thousands of African farmers have commoditized not only their outputs, but also their inputs in the form of hired labour. Therefore in many rural communities one can find small-capitalist farmers and the beginnings of proletarianization. In the next chapter we consider hired labour, migrant workers, 'semi-proletarianization' and capitalist production as part of contemporary farming in tropical Africa.

4

AGRICULTURAL LABOURERS, SHARE-CROPPERS AND MIGRANT WORKERS

The mobilization of labour for commercial agriculture has led to new production relationships and has required high levels of seasonal and permanent migration. Labour mobility is essential where labour-intensive agriculture obtains and when the development of capitalist relations of production has been less than complete. Frequently men enter into wage-paid occupations on a seasonal, periodic, or temporary basis and their employment is often characterized by a whole range of contractual arrangements. Farm workers may be paid in cash by the day, or by the job, and there are systems of shared crops, shared time, combinations of cash and payment in kind, and the rights to use land; furthermore, all these forms may co-exist within a region, or even within a village. Those involved in seasonal or periodic labour circulation are rarely completely separated from access to the means of production, and they are not totally dependent on a wage for their livelihoods. Hired farm workers are not easily fitted into the category of 'wage labour' and they are often referred to as 'semi-proletarians' or 'semi-peasants'. Investigations of rural wage labour have not been prominent in the study of African workers, and there has been a reluctance to grapple with situations where categorization is difficult, and where African labour is employed by African capital. Attention has more often been focussed on those employed in mines and on railways, although they are greatly outnumbered by those working as hired farm labourers, who have been important in the expansion of capitalist agriculture in Ghana, Kenya, Nigeria, Senegal, the Gambia, Tanzania and Uganda.

Rural communities in many parts of Africa now contain those who are neither urban folk nor peasants; they display a heterogeneity which is symptomatic of the shift towards the commoditization of the economy. Rural communities contain agricultural wage labourers, 'semi-proletarians' whose sustenance depends in part upon the sale or barter of their labour, and those who work occasionally to accumulate cash to invest in their farms, or non-farm enterprises, or to pay off debts. In addition there are peasants, small-capitalist farmers and landless workers. The presence of such diverse categories affects the specification of 'peasant' communities and the boundaries which separate them are often fuzzy and may lack permanence over relatively short periods of time. Landless workers may be concealed as they are still part of kinship networks which have access to land, and there are full-time and part-time wage labourers who are part of farming households: also it is important to distinguish between land-rich and land-poor, and labour-rich and labour-poor domestic groups. What we are confronting is a situation where the rural economy encompasses different sectors and where none is fully interpretable without reference to the others (Mintz, 1979).

The less-than-complete transformation of indigenous economies to fully-fledged capitalist relations of production has given rise to a variety of explanations, including dependency theory, peripheral capitalism and the articulation of modes of production. The continuance of peasantries, or small-scale commodity producers, together with the seasonal circulation of labour rather than the development of a substantial and relatively permanent wage labour force have become predominant issues in development studies. Those interested in the articulation or linkage of non-capitalist and capitalist modes of production have argued that the penetration of capitalist forms of production has depended on migrant labour being supported by the home areas to which they periodically return, while the reproduction of peasant labour relies on the continued element of subsistence in farming households. This process of partial reproduction and partial dissolution of pre-capitalist economies has best fitted the interest of capitalist relations of production, especially when geared to external markets. The process was particularly apparent under colonialism, although it has continued since, but with a reduced element of coercion. The articulation argument is more appropriate when dealing with wage labour in the mines and plantations of East and South Africa, but is open to qualification when dealing with those areas where labour contracts and payments have a greater element of mutual advantage to both hirer and hired. In any case, the outcome of the articulation of capitalist and pre-capitalist modes and configurations of capitalist relations would depend very much on the non-capitalist forms encountered in different parts of Africa. In some areas capitalist penetration led to the re-shaping or adaptation of indigenous institutions, such as domestic slavery, communal labour and other forms of labour exchange. This has been referred to as 'restructuration' (Balandier, 1963) and we shall return to this later in this chapter, as well as in Chapter 5.

But if households and migrant workers partly reproduce their own labour power and allow the payment of low wages, then the household also gives workers the possibility of withdrawing from wage labour, if wages and conditions of employment become too poor. Workers can withdraw into subsistence agriculture or small-scale commercial farming at home. Similarly small-scale commodity producers may temporarily withdraw from production for the market, or shift from one crop to another if prices become too low, and cases of this have occurred in the groundnut industry in Senegal, the Gambia and Nigeria, as well as in cocoa production in Ghana; farmers have either suspended commercial crop production and retreated into subsistence, or moved into commercial food production. Therefore, 'proletarianization' and 'peasantization' are not irreversible processes as long as the majority of workers are not separated from their own means of production (Cruise O'Brien, 1979; Jeng, 1978; Van Hear, 1982).

In this chapter we shall look at the increased use of hired labour as small-scale commodity production has moved towards small-scale capitalist farming. As we have already stressed, the use of hired labour may be intermittent, and we shall begin by looking at the seasonal use and deployment of hired labour by farmers engaged primarily in growing export crops. Next we turn our attention to agriculture around towns, where there is a growing market for food staples which is in part being met by farmers who employ considerable amounts of hired labour. It is around towns and in their hinterlands that capitalist relations of production in agriculture and 'proletarianization' may have become most advanced: in addition it is where members of farming households may have become part of the urban workforce. But in the rural sector the hiring of labour from outside the domestic group may take many forms, and for this reason some discussion of shared-contract employment is necessary. Finally, we make some reference to labour migration, since the development of wage and shared-contract labour has created a highly-mobile labour force leading to the redistribution of workers on a regional and international scale.

HIRED LABOUR: ITS SEASONAL USE AND DEPLOYMENT

Farm surveys of hired labour tend to be couched in terms of aggregate inputs or monthly averages for specific crops, with export crops receiving most attention, and less being said about hired labour for commercial food staples, or subsistence crops. Also, hired labour is frequently undifferentiated, and may even include non-household reciprocal labour. Information about the use of hired labour within villages, and between households, and the mobilization of locally-hired labour is even less well studied. The reluctance to study African labour employed by Africans may be influenced by the fact that it is not the easiest of jobs to document and separate out day-by-day the various types of hired labour, and to determine the sources and origins of hired workers, other than by crude categories such as local and non-local, or by nationality. Given these qualifications we can now look at some empirical data on the amounts of hired labour used in farming, its application, sources and users.

Hired labour has become especially important in those areas where production for the market has developed most; as we saw in the last chapter, bottlenecks in the labour supply and the clash of interests between cash and food crops have led farmers to resort to several methods of easing these constraints. Farm surveys have shown that the proportion of hired labour can be very high, for example Galletti *et al.* (1956) found that in the cocoa belt of south-western Nigeria on average 41 per cent of farm labour used for cocoa was hired, while in some instances it reached proportions of 78 per cent. The frequency graph in Figure 4.1 shows the seasonal relationship of different labour operations and the monthly changes in labour use, indicating the proportion done by household labour. The impression is of a fairly even input of household labour, with hired workers being conspicuously used to overcome the seasonal pressures imposed by certain jobs.

But this generalized frequency graph hides the considerable variation found within the cocoa belt, because villages combine different food crops with cocoa, which means that

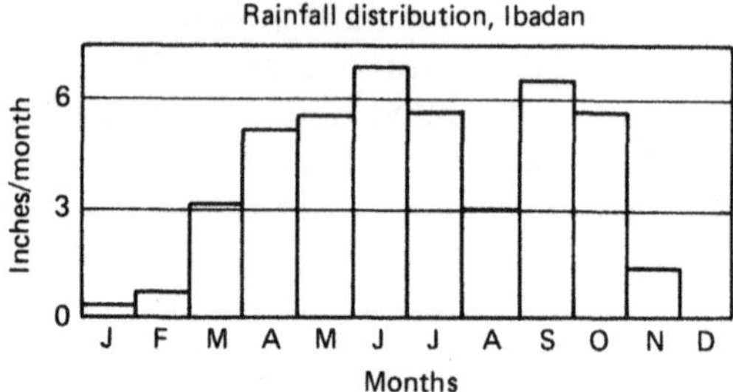

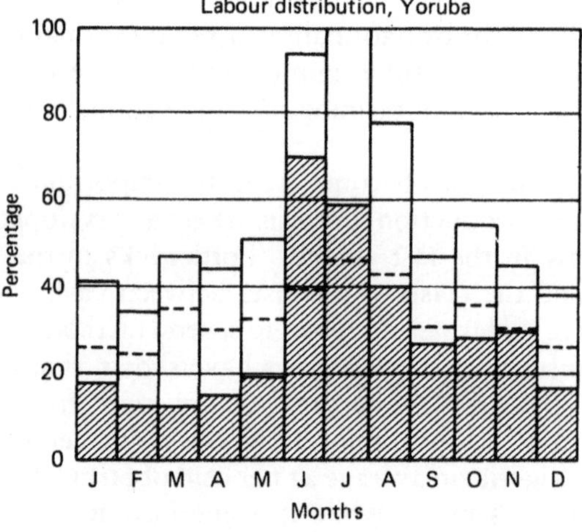

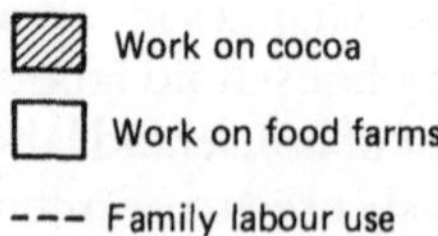

Fig. 4.1 The seasonal distribution of labour: cocoa farms, Nigeria. *Source:* Galletti *et al.* (1956); Cleave (1974), p. 78.

competition for labour on cocoa and food staples changes from place to place. Rice, cassava and yams comprise the basic foodstuffs and those farmers growing rice require less hired labour than those dependent on yams as their principal food staple. Table 4.1 gives a good impression of the differences in the amounts of labour hired and food staples grown by cocoa farmers in Ghana and Nigeria. Thus the absolute and relative sizes of the food and cocoa sectors and the type of foodstuffs are important in determining the seasonal patterns of labour and labour hiring. Similar patterns of seasonal labour hiring were found in Tanzania among cotton growers who were cultivating maize, beans and groundnuts as food staples. The weeding and planting of food crops from December to January coincided with cotton planting, which begins in late December; farmers could not manage without resorting to hired labour, and on average each farm employed 52 man-days (Collinson, cited in Cleave, 1974).

The introduction of commercial crops in some instances extends the limited growing season and may help to even out farm workloads. In north-western Nigeria in Sokoto state the basic food complex is sorghum, millet, cowpeas with groundnuts and cotton if the climate is wet enough. Rainfall varies from 40 inches (1,000 mm) in the south of the state to 25 inches (625 mm) in the north, which allows the cultivation of cotton in the southern sector. Luning (1967) has shown that farms in the cotton-growing areas have higher levels of farm activity as cotton planting succeeds millet and the cotton harvest is not finished until December. As Figure 4.2 shows, the input of family labour continues for a longer period on southern farms, but additional labour for cotton harvesting is taken from the northern farming areas, where the long dry season contributes to the pronounced seasonal migration of workers, into commercial farming areas and towns, as farmers look for employment.

Table 4.1 *West African cocoa villages: relative areas and labour use per farm*

Village and number of farms		Food crops			Bearing cocoa				
						Labour per acre		Cocoa yields	
		Main	Second	Area (acres)	Area (acres)	Total hours	Hired hours	lbs/acre	lbs/hr
Ibesse	10	Cassava	Rice	5.5	5.6	130	64	397	3.1
Mamu	19	Cassava	Yams	2.8	2.8	380	129	307	0.8
Gbongan	21	Yams	Cassava	4.5	9.9	160	125	331	1.4
Oshu	15	Yams	Maize	2.0	1.2	671	375	304	0.5
Akokoaso	10	Plantain	Cocoyam	4.5	2.8	200	25	416	2.0

Sources: Galletti *et al.* (1956), tables XLI, XLII, XLIII; Beckett (1944), pp. 67, 80; Cleave (1974), p. 81.

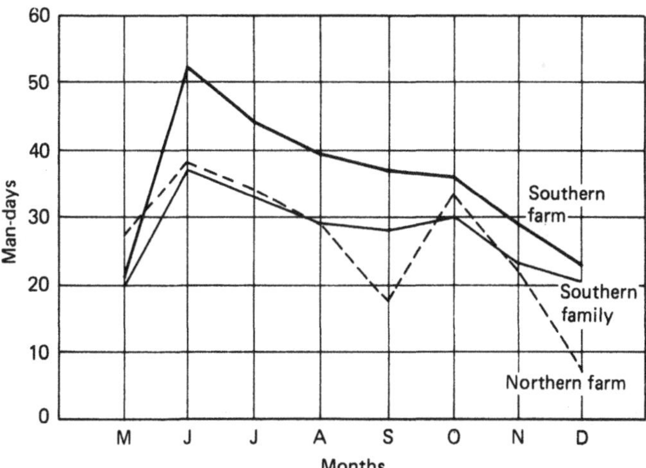

Fig. 4.2 The seasonal distribution of labour: groundnut farms, Sokoto, northern Nigeria. Employment (including hired labour) on standard $7\frac{1}{2}$-acre farms.

Sources: Luning (1967), p. 83; Cleave (1974), p. 108.

Figure 4.2 also shows the distribution of labour and the time spent on non-farm labour and minor farm work, which cover employment in crafts, labouring in towns and the cultivation of rice flood-cover land and dry-season-irrigated farms.

The data collected from Sokoto by Luning show a decline in non-farm work as the labour peak for upland farming of sorghum and millet approaches. In more recent times, from the 1970s onwards, farmers have changed the extent to which they reduce their involvement in non-farm work during the period when farming activity is maximized. Norman's study of three Nigerian villages near Zaria showed on average that 29 per cent of farm labour came from non-household sources, and was employed throughout the year on upland farms growing millet and sorghum and irrigated farms growing onions and vegetables. The labour employed in the Zaria villages came from poorer households with less land, or from those with surplus labour, which was employed on a casual basis for short periods and paid by the hour on a piece-work basis. Continuous use of hired labour reflects the long history of irrigated farming in parts of Hausaland and the market potential of an area of high population density and a well-established urban system. In the Zaria villages many domestic groups had members working in non-farm jobs who continued working throughout the year even at the peak labour season in June and July (Norman, 1972).

The proximity of villages to towns is an important element in their patterns of farming, and of farm and non-farm employment. In some parts of Africa, such as the Sudanic belt of West Africa, urban–rural relations displayed a good deal of complexity and interaction in pre-colonial times. But with the rapid growth of urban centres throughout the sub-continent, urban peripheries have become important areas of social and economic change, and the differentiation of farming households has proceeded at a rate which equals, if not exceeds, that of the older commercial cropping zones. It may be appropriate to think of the cash-crop revolution being succeeded by an agricultural revolution in the peri-urban fringes of African towns. The seasonal hiring of labour continues in areas growing export crops, but they are paralleled by urban peripheries where farm labour is hired continuously. This is a function of the urban market for foodstuffs, and of the opportunities for farmers to engage in urban employment and trading, while replacing or supplementing domestic labour by hired labour.

HIRED LABOUR: URBAN PERIPHERIES AND HINTERLANDS

The pre-colonial towns of Africa, such as those of the Yoruba in south-western Nigeria, had highly centralized systems of administration and a well-developed social division of labour, and were centres of trading networks; they also had populations who farmed the land around the town up to distances of some 50 kms. Urban farmers are a continuing feature of Yorubaland and kin-based domestic groups may subdivide, with some members spending the majority of their time in town while others remain in the countryside. Rural–urban links also result from the fission of large town compounds and the creation of satellite rural households, with labour being redistributed daily or seasonally between town and village compounds within a particular kinship grouping (S. Goddard, 1965; Watts, 1980). Marginal applications of labour for weeding and harvesting can be contrived through short-term movements of labour within the extended groups, which are spatially divided between town and countryside.

As might be expected, these bi-local arrangements are susceptible to rapid change and re-orientation, as the more 'traditional' arrangements are modified. Olusanya (1972) observed that, although some urban farmers may spend a day, a few days or a few months on their farm, over the years the development of permanent outlying villages and a more complete fission of households has occurred. This is a product of rising population densities, a more intensive use of land, individuation and the erosion of large farming households. But this phase has been succeeded by a more recent one as villagers are moving back into the towns. In parts of the north-west of the former Western State, there has been an influx of migrant farmers from the savannah area to the north, who have become tenant farmers or hired labourers. A survey of the landlords of tenants showed that 35 per cent of them had a permanent base in town and they were using tenant and hired labour to keep their farmland in use while they were taking alternative jobs in the urban sector.

Although some attention has been focussed on urban farmers, little investigation has been made of the farming activities of those who are primarily engaged in the small-scale manufacturing and service sector. In work carried out in the Gambia, several kinds of labour movements were observed whereby urban traders and small-scale businessmen engaged in wet-season farming (Swindell, 1980). In one village some five miles from the up-river town of Basse one compound was a temporary homestead of a town trader and his family who farmed groundnuts in the wet season, after which he moved back to town in the dry season, using the proceeds of groundnut sales to contribute to trading stock. This seasonal switch from the service to the agricultural sector is a strategy which is symptomatic of an economy which undergoes seasonal fluctuations, low levels of capital accumulation and imperfect job specialization leading to seasonal and daily circulation of labour.

But for many villagers who live near towns it is commonplace that one or more members of the farming household have permanent town jobs, travelling to and from work daily, and working on farms during the evenings and weekends. Under such conditions, the absence of household members working in town may generate the replacement of their labour at peak times during the farming cycle, or permanently by hired labourers who may be drawn from poorer farmers within the village, from unemployed urban workers, or even from long-distance labour migrants. Therefore local daily migration, and long-distance seasonal migration may be complementary. Within the rural–urban fringe one suspects the existence of a development sequence of migration types and transitional forms of mobility.

Seasonal work in the town may be a prelude to a more permanent employment, which if successful leaves a niche for longer-distance migrants to move into the villages in the peri-urban fringe, who in their turn may find urban employment on a seasonal basis when not required on the farm.

In 1979 the author was working in a village some four miles from Sokoto in modern Nigeria, where prosperous farming households had men who were full-time workers in the government sector (for example, as carpenters in the Public Works Department), who hired long-distance migrants (from Niger) to tend animals and draw water in the dry season. These men were paid by the 'stick', that is a wooden yoke supporting two four-gallon kerosene cans, and they earned about 2–3 Naira per day (₦ 1.00 approximately equals £0.80). Farm workers were also hired during the wet season, who came from other villages up to 20 miles (33 km) away, attracted by the higher wages for farm work in the peri-urban villages. Farm workers were being paid ₦ 3–4.00 per day, which was about equivalent to the daily wage-rate paid for the lowest grade worker in the government sector, or on private construction sites; in 1979 the minimum government wage was ₦ 100.00 per month. In 1982–3, Sutherland (1983), working in other villages in the Sokoto periphery, found that men were paid from ₦ 3–5.00 per day for cutting crop residues, while for watering irrigated farmland in the dry season, a particularly labour-intensive job, rates could be as much as ₦ 6.00 per day (1982–3 government minimum wage: ₦ 120 per month). The rates paid to farm labourers varied with the job and from season to season, and of course, compared with work in the government sector, it was seasonal and lacked security. However, the amount of hiring was considerable, and in one village close to Sokoto, Sutherland found that every compound had at least one member who was hiring labour for their farms.

Farm wages in the urban periphery have been pushed up by the competition from the government sector and the construction industry for unskilled labour, and is a reflection of the rapid urbanization which took place in Nigeria from 1975 to 1979, associated with the oil boom and the development of new State capitals and Local Government Headquarter towns. But in other parts of Africa, and in earlier periods, wage-rates in urban peripheries have shown a differential from those of remoter areas. The Farm Enterprise Survey in Kenya, 1970–1, indicated a complex pattern of farm wages, as in some high-density areas of intensive farming, and in areas close to alternative urban employment, casual wage-rates of 3.0 to 3.9 Kenyan shillings per day were offered, compared with 1.5 to 2.7 in other areas (see Kongstad and Mönsted, 1980).

There also seems to be some evidence that the 'middle' and 'poorer peasantry' within urban peripheries have become more dependent for their incomes on the 'formal' and 'informal' sectors of nearby towns, to the extent that their farms have become subsidiary parts of the sustenance and reproduction of their households. On the other hand richer peasants have also become involved in urban employment and trading, but at the same time maintaining their farms by using hired labour, often producing foodstuffs for the urban market. In a study of two villages near Kano in Nigeria, Amerena (1982) found that 31 and 34 per cent of farmers participated in non-farm occupations in both the wet and dry seasons, but between 64.9 and 90 per cent of them put non-farm work as their chief source of cash income; these farmers had become 'semi-peasants', who relied on younger members and wives to run their farms, while the 'big-men' of the village hired-in wage labour. A study of PAYE tax returns for the two villages showed that up to 34 per cent of males in some villages were employed in the 'formal' large-scale commercial and industrial sector. It was also apparent that participation in all non-farm activities had been given a significant boost by the drought which extended from the late 1960s into the mid-1970s.

Although the majority who live and move within the rural–urban fringes have access to land, irrespective of whether they are primarily urban or rural dwellers, there is an increasing number of landless workers, or land-poor households, in the vicinity of urban settlements. The pressure on land around large African towns can be acute and may originate from within the urban salariat and trading community who are interested in land speculation and building, as well as from rural 'big-men' farmers and traders who wish to increase their landholdings to take advantage of the urban market for food staples (Cohen, 1976; Mortimore and Wilson, 1965; Mortimore, 1975). The result is that small-scale farmers may be squeezed and sell land, and they are especially vulnerable if the household is at a point in its developmental cycle where there is an adverse dependency ratio; if this is combined with illness, debt, or bad harvests, then the sale of land may become inevitable. This process produces landless workers, or those from non-viable farming households who move between town and countryside in response to daily or seasonal opportunities for work. It is this kind of worker who may be mobilized as gang-labour on the bigger farms in the rural areas, as well as forming the nucleus of a permanent wage labour force in the town. Usually such workers live in rented accommodation in the suburbs and are part of the shift towards capitalist farming and 'proletarianization', a process which is accentuated around many African cities.

Examples of these processes can be found in diverse locations: around towns set amidst areas of high and low population density, around towns which have long pre-colonial régimes. However, the impact of large towns is particularly apparent. We have already referred to the towns of Hausaland in northern Nigeria, the most important of which – Kano, Zaria, Katsina, and Sokoto – have notable pre-colonial histories and are surrounded by areas of intensive cultivation and high population densities. Land tenure is a complex mixture of Islamic law and customary law, the former being strongest close to the town, whereas the latter becomes more important with increasing distance (Bijimi, 1963). Land is inherited, given by District Heads, loaned, rented or purchased. The purchase of land is not new, and in 1860 the Sultan of Sokoto put a stop to the sale of houses and land; but by 1881 it was re-established, and by the 1930s the colonial officers' district notebooks contain abundant evidence of sale of land. In 1967–8, Goddard *et al.* (1971) found that in the periphery of Sokoto between 19 and 29 per cent of land had been acquired by purchase in the three villages they studied; land leased or loaned amounted to between 2.8 and 12 per cent. Similar observations have been made around Kano, Katsina and Zaria; in the case of the latter, in 1965–6 some 18 per cent of land in the surrounding districts was loaned or rented and 5.8 per cent acquired by purchase (Davies, 1976). The purchase of peri-urban land from the mid-1970s onwards had been exacerbated by the oil boom in Nigeria and the 1978 Land Decree, which has increased private investment in land and State spending on the extension of Government Residential Areas' land for schools, colleges, universities and administrative buildings (Main, 1981; Sutherland, 1983).

In Central Africa, the towns of the former Franco-Belgian territories are much more recent creations, and they have experienced both similar and dissimilar processes of agrarian change in their peri-urban fringes. Bangui (approximately 200,000 inhabitants) in the Central African Republic is surrounded by a belt of market gardens developed on marshlands which allow cultivation to continue throughout the dry season from December to February. The produce is for a relatively limited market comprising upper- and middle-class town dwellers, richer merchants, the European sector and institutions such as colleges and hospitals. Unlike the Hausa towns, these market gardens are run by rural immigrants of diverse ethnic origins, but who have generally come from those parts where commercial farming is least developed, or where the environment is less good. The farms of these migrants are paralleled by those operated by large commercial firms using hired labour as well as government-operated schemes using tenant farmers (Prioul, 1969).

Pointe Noire in the Congo Republic is another recent city which has a surrounding belt of market gardening, partly developed by migrants. The city is surrounded by areas of low population density and poor farmland; food has to be brought from considerable distances, which increases its cost; consequently many poorer urban dwellers have taken to farming the periphery to grow at least part of their food requirements. The shift back to farming by urban dwellers was given another push when the capital was moved from Pointe Noire to Brazzaville, with the subsequent loss of jobs, and many of those formerly employed in the government sector moved into peripheral farming for the urban market rather than moving elsewhere (Vennetier, 1961). This is an example of the contention that 'proletarianization' is not so intrenched as to be irreversible; it also reflects the way in which labour even in the 'formal' sector can be quickly shed in the absence of unionization, or other forms of labour organization.

Large towns have an impact which extends well beyond their immediate peripheries, stretching out along the principal axes of communication. Urban hinterlands provide food and fuel and the feeding of large urban populations has become an important issue for many governments, which has been resolved by a variety of agricultural schemes, or by food imports. Kinshasa in Zaire has a population of some two million and the area known as Lower Zaire provides some 55 per cent of the city's cassava, 90 per cent of its vegetables and 90 per cent of its charcoal. Prices for food are high and many peasant farmers in Lower Zaire are now integrated into the market economy directed towards Kinshasa.

In the Kinshasa periphery there is considerable pressure on land for building as the town expands, and both the laws of 1963 and 1973 prohibiting the sale of communal farmland have been ignored. An intensive zone of cultivation extends outwards from the edge of the city for about 10 kms, the development of which has been greatly influenced by urban dwellers. In the first instance members of the urban bourgeoisie bought up bush and forest, in blocks of between 50–200 ha, from local chiefs, for use as firewood. Once the bush had been cleared, then the next stage was the cultivation of cassava and fruits for the Kinshasa market using young unemployed or underemployed labour recruited in the city. Village land round Kinshasa and in Lower Zaire has also been reduced by sugar plantations set up in the colonial period, and more recently by the establishment of cattle ranches by urban capitalist farmers (Kayser *et al.*, 1981). The penetration by urban capital of the periphery around Kinshasa has been made relatively easy by low population densities, hitherto extensive bush-fallow cultivation, and the power of urban interest groups, which has rendered ineffective the legislation introduced to prevent the alienation of land.

SHARE-CONTRACTS

So far we have been interested chiefly in the use of wage labour, but the hiring of extra labour by means of crop-sharing, or giving land in lieu of wages and payments, has a long history, and is by no means finished. Share-contracts are widespread, not only in Africa but throughout the tropical world, where they have been particularly important in the development of export crops. From a theoretical stand-point these methods of organizing labour and land have been dismissed as inefficient, semi-feudal and a prelude to more capitalist systems of rents and wage labour. 'Traditional' or neo-classical critics have pointed to the lack of incentive, on the part of both tenant and landlord, to invest resources to bring productivity up to the levels which could obtain under owner-occupation or fixed rents. The issues raised by neo-classical analyses are the competitiveness of the bargaining procedure, the variability of the rental share, the comparative productivity of different contractual arrangements and the implications for landlord and tenant investment (Pearce, 1983). Yet such systems persist, and they have been immensely important in the development of export crops by African farmers. Share-contract labour has been used to realize levels of input intensity and output little different from allegedly more efficient forms of organization (Robertson, 1982).

One of the problems encountered when discussing share-cropping is the use of the term to describe a whole range of contractual circumstances; indeed, as we shall see later, it is not just land and crop which are shared, but labour, and for this reason we shall use the term share-contract. In essence share-contracts refer to situations where access to some necessary factor of production is provided for by one party, in return for either a pre-arranged proportion of the crop, or some other factor. In the latter cases land may be exchanged for labour and vice versa. But it has been suggested by Pearce (1983) that the crux of the share-contract is its being a mechanism whereby owners of the means of production (landlords) acquire access to others' labour.

From a theoretical standpoint, it can be asked under what conditions do share-contracts become the preferred form of surplus labour appropriation, how do their production relationships relate to the nature and pace of agricultural change, and if they persist, are they subject to increasingly stringent control by the interests of the hirer? These issues have been discussed at some length by Pearce (1983) and some of his conclusions seem pertinent to the African case; for example he suggests that share-contracts may be preferred where the tenant is in a position to have a decisive influence upon the contract, and where class relations between landlords and tenants are less obviously determined.

In the African context landlords are frequently not the owners of land; they have use-rights, many are small-commodity producers not capitalist farmers, and the labourer may well be in a position to make a contract on good terms. We can add that production is built around household labour, with extra workers needed only at specific points in the cultivation cycle, but in the absence of a well-developed labour market a supply of casual labour may not be available at these times. Share-contracts allow the farmer to have labour 'on-tap' within his compound, which fits in with farming systems where labour inputs are variable and timing is vital. Share-contracts might be expected to hold up well where population densities are relatively low and land is available; they also avoid the need for cash payments in households where levels of capital accumulation are of a low order. From the labourer's point of view he is provided with food as well as land under most contracts and his position in households can be little different (some would say better) from that of junior members of the household who have limited access to land and its product.

Historically, there is much to suggest that share-contracts emerge from more complete forms of labour control, such as slavery in the southern United States, villeinage in Europe and forms of domestic slavery in Africa. Thus share-cropping may be seen as an intermediate stage between forms of agrestic servitude and the full commoditization of rural labour itself. This contemporary occurrence and persistence of share-contracts underlines the contention that the transformation of African agriculture is taking place differentially over space and time: it may be that share-contracts are consistent with capitalist relations in their early stages of development, that is, when non-capitalist labour processes are subsumed under capitalist relations.

Share-contracts display a good deal of variation and flexibility and it is not possible to examine all the areas where such arrangements are used; instead, examples will be taken from cocoa farming in Ghana and groundnut farming in Senegal and the Gambia. Both these countries have long histories of export crop production and local farmers have had to recruit large amounts of hired labour in order to expand the production of cocoa and groundnuts. Labour is hired by means of share-contracts, as well as wages, although the former has shown a remarkable resilience to change and in certain circumstances has actually strengthened. Different forms of hired labour can operate simultaneously in a particular village or area, and the shift from one form to another is not always from share-contracts to wages.

In the early years of the twentieth century the Gold Coast experienced high levels of capital investment by Europeans, especially in gold mines, railways and roads. Almost at the same time there was a spectacular expansion of the cocoa industry, which had started in the 1890s, by Africans buying and investing money accumulated from palm-oil trading. Farmers from the Akwapim ridge began to colonize sparsely-settled areas to the west; later they were joined by others and soon after 1900 there was a westward migration and a scramble for land (Hill, 1963). Many peasant farmers became involved in cocoa farming, and the returns were such that they resisted attempts to be recruited into mines, as carriers and as plantation workers, preferring small-scale commodity production, because it was more lucrative than wage labour, and more subject to their personal control. In the early years it appears that hired labour played a small part in establishing cocoa farms, but after 1900 the demand for labour increased as domestic groups could not manage to clear new farms and maintain and harvest those coming into fruit.

In the first instance, labourers were hired as annual contract workers, who were used to establish new farms and were housed, clothed and fed during the contract, and at the end paid a lump sum in cash. Alternatively, sharecroppers were employed, on the basis of their receiving one-third of the crop and they became known as *abusa* men (*abusa*, Twi for one-third): in addition they were given land on which they cultivated food. As well as labourers for cocoa cultivation, farmers hired large numbers of carriers to take their produce to the European merchant firms, a practice which had been used in the pre-colonial period when the palm-oil trade was so important. *Abusa* labourers were hired to establish new crops and tend existing ones and were also responsible for carrying the crop to market. A variation on this system was *nkotokuano* labourers, who weeded, harvested, dried and fermented cocoa, but did not carry it. They were paid a proportion of the price realized for each load, which varied between one-eighth and one-fifth. *Abusa*, *nkotokuano* and annual contracts were the forms of hiring associated with the development of the cocoa industry, together with casual labourers who worked for a daily wage or agreed amount for a specific job.

Van Hear (1982) has admirably charted the development of agricultural labour in Ghana, which included the changing conditions of employment in the cocoa industry and the struggles between African labour and capital. All the forms of employment enumerated above still obtain, but their relative importance has altered, as have the forms of contract. After 1946 there was an increase in annual-contract workers who were paid between £5 and £8 per contract, but as farmers became increasingly devious over the payment of workers, *abusa* contracts became preferred; also under share-cropping a rise in the price of cocoa benefits both farmers and labourers. Thus after 1946 there was a shift towards share-cropping among experienced cocoa labourers in the south as they perceived its advantages. On the other hand, employers of labour reacted by using labour recruiters and collectors (albeit illegally) to bring workers from northern Ghana as annual-contract workers; in addition they tightened up *abusa* contracts by making labourers work food-farms in their spare time, or charging a fee as a contribution to their maintenance. In these ways farmers attempted to increase the surplus value they could extract from the contracts. At the same time casual day labour increased against annual contracts as labourers found this system more lucrative, flexible and subject to bargaining over rates of pay and the length of the working day.

From the mid 1950s onwards farm labour became scarce in Ghana as a result of changes in the agricultural sector and the competition for labour from other sectors. Commercial food-farming was already established in northern Ashanti and it was further developed in the north by the State in an attempt to redress the economic imbalance between north and south. Furthermore, the State sector began to absorb more labour, the timber industry expanded, and there was a general drift of young men into the towns. The situation was further exacerbated by the expulsion of aliens in 1969, a measure which particularly affected the supply of foreign migrant labour to the cocoa areas (Peil, 1974). At the same time, the prices of cocoa began to plummet and by 1972 the cocoa industry was stagnating. Labourers pressed for higher wages under daily and piece-rate systems and bigger farmers began to resort to contractors who would undertake to do farm work at an agreed rate and then hire the labourers. By the mid-1950s a class of farm labourers had emerged, and a class of capitalist farmers who had become increasingly reliant upon hired labour and who assumed the role of farm managers. Although share-contracts are still used, they have not had the same importance in commercial food-farming as cocoa, and the increased polarization of capitalist farmers and hired labourers has undercut both share- and annual contracts.

The groundnut industry of Senegal and the Gambia (the Senegambian Federation since 1982) began as far back as 1830, when European merchant capital began to look for alternative sources of investment, as the slave trade had virtually ceased. The result was the setting-up of trading stations along the coast and principal rivers, especially the Gambia River, to encourage local farmers to produce groundnuts alongside their millet and sorghum. Eventually, under colonial influence in the late nineteenth and early twentieth centuries, areas of specialization developed, for example, in the hinterland of Dakar, in Cayor and Baol which became known as the peanut basin. Farmers had to intensify the use of their domestic labour and alter the internal division of labour; but also they had to use external sources and the industry mobilized large numbers of migrant workers from within the Senegambian basin, as well as from the interior regions of the upper Niger in Mali and eventually from Guinea. These workers were hired not on a share-cropping arrangement but on a shared-land, shared-time system, and the participants became known as Strange Farmers in the Gambia, and *Navétanes* in Senegal. Numbers reached over 100,000 in the 1930s; since then they have dwindled in Senegal, although they remain an important element in extending the frontiers and marginal areas of groundnut cultivation, but they have persisted in the Gambia (Swindell, 1978; Colvin *et al.*, 1981).

The Strange Farmer contract is based on the host giving the worker a piece of land on which he can cultivate his own groundnuts in return for three or four days' labour on the host's farms. The worker, usually a migrant, splits his time between his own farm plot and that of his host; in addition the host provides food, housing and tools, while the labourer may contribute a tenth of his groundnut crop. The number of days worked, the length of the working day, access to the host's ox-plough and co-operative, and the payment of a percentage of the labourer's crop are all negotiable, and vary according to whether the worker has become a regular Strange Farmer within a particular household over a number of years. Hosts can give better or poorer land, and more or less accessible land, as payments to their Strange Farmers, which may affect the returns to their labour in conjunction with hours worked. The stranger's chief security is the knowledge that his crop of groundnuts will accrue to him alone, and can be converted into cash at the end of the season.

The arrangements between host and labourer can move in favour of one or the other; in some areas strangers work fewer days, while in some cases hosts also help on their strangers' farms. But in essence the host is trying to mobilize extra labour, appropriate a surplus and pay for it without using cash in a cultivation system where timing of labour inputs for groundnuts is vital. Yields drop considerably if planting and weeding are delayed, while late harvesting reduces yields, as groundnuts become more difficult to lift as the soil hardens as the dry season progresses. The Strange Farmer system has been of immense importance in the development of the groundnut trade, and it now persists where population densities remain fairly low and there is still surplus land over labour; also where alternative wage employment in the wet season is limited. The reduced significance of this type of share-contract in the older areas of Baol and Cayor in the Dakar hinterland has been due to the competition for labour in Dakar and other regional towns, migrant employment to France, and high population densities which have made land increasingly scarce. Groundnut farmers have made increased use of casual day-labour and paid gang-labour as the labour market has grown and farming has become more capitalized by the use of the ox plough and of weeders. But it must be emphasized that in many villages one can find Strange Farmers, daily-paid labour, communal labour and paid gang-labour co-existing in differing proportions, with the richer farmers employing all these different types. The Strange Farmer contract is preferred because it reduces the risk of being without labour at critical times in the cultivation cycle, and employers know that the recruitment of daily labour or contract workers is very difficult to achieve at short notice when the labour market is poorly developed.

As to the origins of this form of hired labour, it would seem that it has developed from domestic slavery, which began to decay towards the end of the nineteenth century. After the ending of the Atlantic slave trade and development of groundnut farming domestic slaves became valuable as farm labourers rather than commodities, and together with migrant farmers they formed the bulk of the labour force. But throughout the Sudanic zone of West Africa, Islamic law and practice gave slaves certain rights, not least of which was access to farm plots of their own, with a specified number of days on which they could work them. The parallel between the Strange Farmer system and these arrangements is obvious, and with the erosion of slavery and the passing of Slave Abolition Ordinances in the 1890s, farmers took on farm labourers on a pattern of shared-time with which they familiar. But the difference was that now ex-slaves had freedom of movement, the labour force became more mobile, and the numbers of migrant workers increased as the groundnut trade expanded under colonial rule. The early migrant workers of the 1850s were either freemen farmers, or gangs of slaves brought down to the Gambia River by merchants from the interior, and rents were paid to local rulers for the use of land. The Strange Farmer system as such really took off when slavery declined (Swindell, 1978).

Domestic slavery affected a large proportion of the population of West Africa, in parts of the Sudanic belt possibly between a quarter and a half of the population. This 'reserve' of labour was mobilized as slavery decayed, helped by colonial Abolition Ordinances, as the colonial authorities realized the necessity of a large mobile wage-labour force to develop new transport infrastructures and mines, but most of all agricultural export crops. Abolition and the erosion of domestic slavery, or bonded labour, were just as vital as taxes and the monetization and commoditization of the economy in mobilizing African labour (Swindell, 1984).

AGRICULTURAL LABOUR MIGRATION

Farm labour is recruited locally from within villages and among neighbouring villages, but there are many farm workers who migrate from one region to another and from one country to another. Inter-regional and international migration involves workers in travelling long distances and in prolonged absences from their homes and they have been of tremendous importance in the development of export crops. Labour mobility is notoriously difficult to measure, and few national censuses provide any profound insights, especially when so much agricultural labour migration is seasonal and circulatory. In tropical Africa the number of agricultural long-distance labour migrants may be of the order of two or three million, and there are many more unrecorded local movements of labour. Also, there are many farmers and members of farming households who become seasonal, periodic or long-term migrants in towns, mines and industrial areas, as a means of supporting and reproducing their households back in the village. So far, we have discussed hired labour in the cocoa industry of Ghana and the groundnut industry in Senegal and the Gambia: both these areas have absorbed large numbers of migrant workers, and in the case of Ghana, if its cocoa region is considered along with cocoa and coffee farming in neighbouring Ivory Coast, then we have perhaps the largest zone of in-migration of agricultural workers in tropical Africa. We shall now look at some aspects of migration by cocoa labourers, together with migrants into Senegal and the Gambia, and by way of a contrast, we shall also look at out-migration from rural areas in Kenya to the towns and coffee-growing regions.

The map of migratory movements shown in Fig. 4.3 gives some impression of long-distance labour movements in West Africa and emphasizes the importance of Burkina Faso as a labour reservoir for the Ivory Coast and Ghana. The flow of migrant workers into Ghana was severely curtailed by the Aliens Order of 1969, and in fact subsequently movements out of Ghana have been more conspicuous since the mid-1970s. The declining cocoa industry and an ailing economy has led to an exodus of Ghanaians into Nigeria, attracted by the possibility of employment associated with the 'oil boom'. In 1983 aliens were expelled from Nigeria and the number of Ghanaians removed was estimated at over one million. Burkina Faso remains a major source of West African labour migrants, and in particular the Mossi have played an important role in the development of cocoa- and food-farming in Ghana, and

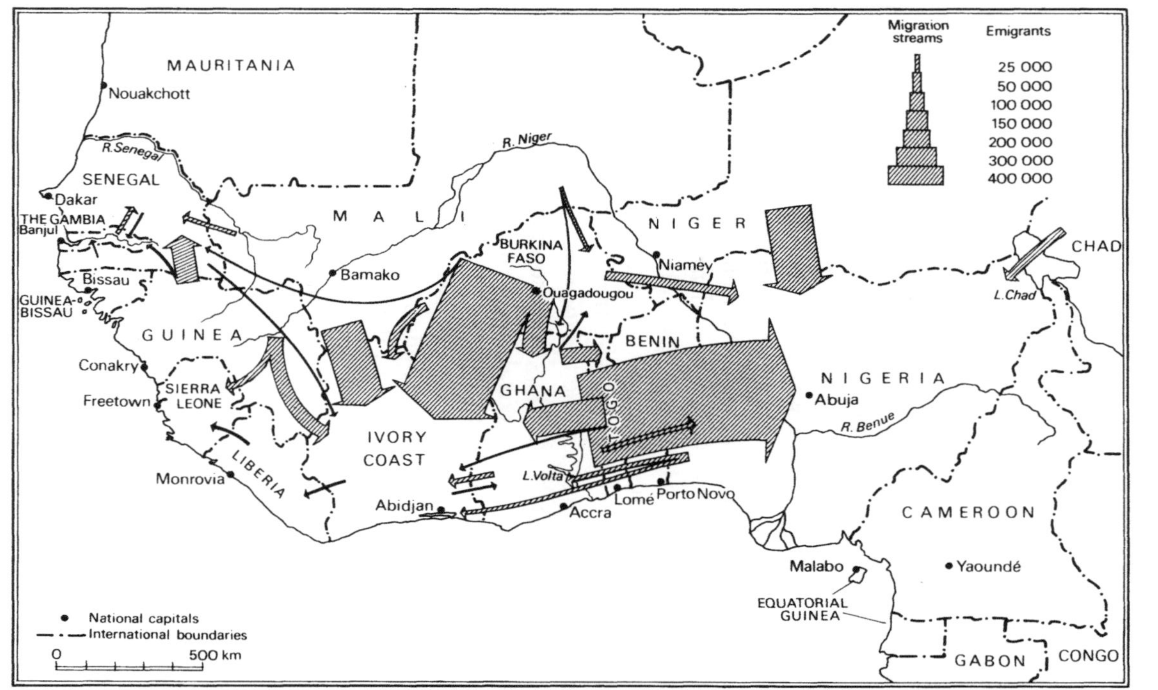

Fig. 4.3 External migration streams in West Africa, based on Zachariah and Condé (1981), together with the author's notional figures for Nigeria.

continue to do so in the Ivory Coast. In 1983 the military government of Burkina Faso tried to curtail the movement of Voltaics by a decree which required travellers to have a *laissez-passer*; so far observers appear to think this has done little to stop outward movements of labour. Annual movements of people from Burkina Faso into the Ivory coast and to a lesser extent Ghana number from between 200,000 and 300,000 per annum.

Labour migrants (particularly annual contract workers) began leaving the Mossi areas at the beginning of the century, a process which was stimulated by the monetization of the economy and the introduction of new taxes by the French which were progressively increased; at the same time little economic growth occurred in the relatively highly populated area of Mossiland. As with northern Ghana, a limited local potential led the colonial régimes to accept these areas as labour reservoirs for the south. Migration has become institutionalized and the incorporation of migrant workers into capitalist farming in the south has become part of their strategy for survival, as well as the means of supplying themselves with an increasing range of commodities. Although forced labour was used, more so in French territories than in Ghana, mobilization of Sudanic labour was brought about primarily by the spread of commodities, the penetration of market relations and the need for cash to satisfy basic needs and supply consumer goods. Many household requirements became commoditized and, in the absence of a flourishing peasant economy at home, the export of household labour was the means whereby goods and bridewealth could be obtained. The continued underdevelopment of the regions of the western Sudan secured the commitment at least of some household members to migrant work, but the commitment was less than complete. Men can, and do, withdraw from migrant labour, either after a period spent away from home, or seasonally. It is of course argued that this is why labour is cheap; it is continually reproduced at home at no cost to employers. On the other hand capitalist farmers do not have access to a secure and committed work force as long as workers are not completely separated from their means of production (Van Hear, 1982).

As we observed above, Ghanaian farmers (and in fact their counterparts in the Ivory Coast) became involved in complex networks for the recruitment of labour, which stimulated regional and international migration. Returning *abusa*-contract men were used to bring back labourers on payment of a commission, while lorry drivers and recruiters became the 'professional' element in the transfer of labour from north to south; the stranger settlements (*zongos*), often with their own resident chiefs, became not only residential areas for migrant workers, but acted as informal labour exchanges for the recruitment and placement of farm workers.

As for the source areas of migrants, there have been inevitable disruptions in the domestic economy, and when migration becomes more than seasonal, and extends for a number of years, the removal of men from villages can be particularly debilitating. During 1973–4, Burkina Faso conducted a National Survey of Migratory Movements to examine the scale of migration, its characteristics, causes and effects. Movements of over three months' duration were recorded for the period 1969–73, which totalled some 700,000 moves, 70 per cent of which were abroad. The survey emphasized the importance of circulatory migration and some 30 per cent of moves were by returnees; about half the moves were from rural to other rural areas. The survey investigated both individual and village attitudes to labour migration, and what the government might do about it. The results showed the ambivalence of opinion; while people know it is beneficial to have a member of their household as a migrant worker, they also know that international migration can, and does, damage the domestic and village economy by the removal of manpower. There was a certain fatalism expressed in the knowledge that Burkina Faso has very limited resources, although informants felt that the government might organize what they had in a better way, as well as providing better information for migrants about jobs and conditions abroad (Coulibaby *et al.*, 1980).

The migration of farm labour into Senegal and the Gambia, to which we referred earlier is almost as old as the groundnut industry itself, and records from the 1850s show that Strange Farmers were coming into the Gambia and travelling from up to 600 miles from the interior (Swindell, 1980). A survey conducted in the Gambia in 1974–5 showed that there were some 33,000 at work during the wet season and that about one-half of the farming households had taken in at least one migrant worker. But the survey also inquired into the previous employment of migrants before arriving on their farms, and of their intentions after they had harvested their groundnuts. This information revealed that about one-half of the migrants had not proceeded directly from their home areas, but had been employed in the previous dry season on a variety of jobs on both the 'informal' and 'formal' sectors, as wage labourers, petty-traders, small-commodity producers and services workers. These jobs were located in the larger towns such as Dakar and Banjul and at river crossings and the groundnut mills (Swindell, 1982). Many farmers intended to repeat this procedure after finishing groundnut farming; thus initial long-distance migration from their homeland to become agricultural workers was extended to include more localized circulation.

The data collected in the survey strongly suggested that there was a transition over time, and that seasonal circulation from home to groundnut farm in the Gambia became extended to include other wage-earning employment, with the period spent away from home becoming longer, although not precluding an ultimate or periodic return after a few years. These movements of labour indicate the complexity of labour mobility and that the degree of 'proletarianization' of labour fluctuates. These migrants in the course of a season shift from share-contract work on groundnut farms to either factory wage labour, or self-employed work, and then over a period of time may move back to the peasant farms from which they originally came. While in the long run there may be a trend towards 'proletarianization' of labour from the less advantaged interior areas of the Sudan, and the poorer sectors of the rural communities in the Gambia, the process is irregular and incomplete. It can be argued that one of the advantages of a seasonal and circulatory migrant labour force is that it provides a flexible reserve, which is particularly appropriate to certain stages of the development of capitalist relations of production. The Strange Farmers fit quite well into the category of a 'floating labour reserve', which serves the interests of small-commodity producers linked to international commodity markets, as well as the industrial sector in the towns.

It has been argued that circulatory labour migration is a necessary part of proletarianization, which in turn is part of the acceleration of capital accumulation (Standing, 1984). Proletarianization is the process whereby the mass of working people become separated from their means of production and become 'free' to sell their labour and develop those attributes, attitudes, commitment and consciousness of a wage–labour force. But proletarianization in Africa and elsewhere has not taken place without resistance, which may be in the form of conflict between labour and capital, or adaptation by peasant farmers to preserve elements of non-capitalist structures. Also, for many circulatory migrants the village remains their social point of reference. The mobilization of labour by means of coercion, taxation and erosion of kin-based domestic structures has been met with resistance of one sort or another, and 'semi-proletarians' seems the most appropriate term for the majority of wage labourers.

The effects of proletarianization have been uncertain, contradictory and by no means uni-directional. The circulation of labour has helped both to preserve and to undermine rural communities and households in the source areas: for example, remittances and goods brought home remove the threat of indebtedness, iron out the effects of bad harvests and put off the sale of land (Standing, 1984). Labour migration may also increase economic differentiation in the areas of out-migration, and, as we observed in Chapter 3, there was evidence from the Kitui region of Kenya that migrants became relatively prosperous and invested their earnings in education for their children, or in their farms (O'Leary, 1983). But the other side of the coin is that poorer households who have men working away from home may benefit in the short run, but in the longer term, if men become caught-up in the nexus of opportunities in the destination areas, the domestic group back home may suffer from the continued loss of their manpower. Much depends on whether remittances combined with farm income are sufficient to offset their absence by hiring-in labour. As we have already seen, one of the effects of commercial production is to alter the internal division of labour in farming households; this process is further exacerbated by outward migration, and the burden of farming falls more and more on women and the aged.

The example of cocoa and groundnut farming has focussed on hirers of migrant labour, but another example from Kenya shows the effects on the source areas and exemplifies some of the points made above about 'proletarianization'. In 1972 O'Keefe, Wisner and Baird studied a village in Kikuyuland in Kenya with particular reference to ecology, land use and underdevelopment. The altitude of the village is such that it is too low for good tea production, but too high for coffee production, the two major cash crops of Kikuyuland. Men from the village migrated to find employment in the towns, while the women took part-time jobs on the coffee estates in order to supplement farm income from landholdings which were in an area of high population density and subject to the interrelated effects of soil erosion and outward labour migration. Some 31 per cent of household heads were absent from the village, returning once a month and on average remitting about 45 per cent of their earnings. It appeared that households with external sources of income (particularly if they were good incomes) tended to accumulate land, while poorer peasants became indebted as they tried to finance taxes and schooling for their children. It is these poorer households who are likely to sell their land, and so shift towards wage employment, but without the ultimate security of their farms.

The withdrawal of men from farming has adversely affected soil conservation, while the option of women doing more work is not available, as they are part-time workers in the downslope coffee estates. This hill region of Kikuyuland did at one time grow coffee, although it was not a good area. The decline in coffee prices adversely affected it, as a marginal producer, which contributed to outward migration leading to a deterioration of the previously terraced hillsides, as well as a failure to interplant the foodstaple, maize, because of inadequate labour. The result is a vicious circle of soil erosion and non-viable farming households who become increasingly 'proletarianized', while a minority become a class of land-owning absentee farmers mainly engaged in urban trading or employment.

The study by O'Keefe *et al.* demonstrates something of the ecological disruption which can occur when a marginal area becomes dependent on labour migration. On the other hand it is not unknown for areas which have served as sources of migrant labour to experience retrenchment; there is the possibility of the 'post-migration' economy. We have spent some time looking at the ways in which African farmers have become producers for the market, at commoditization and 'semi-proletarianization', but the strength and direction of change is subject to fluctuations, even if a general trend is discernible. African economies and political régimes exhibit a fragility which is compounded by changes in the terms of trade for exports and imports, internal *coups* and wars with neighbouring states; all these occurrences can increase the adverse effects of natural hazards such as floods and droughts. In Uganda, during the Amin régime huge expenditures on the army and weaponry depleted foreign exchange reserves, which led to a neglect of the transport system. The decay of systems of collection and distribution adversely affected cotton, coffee and sugar production as well as inflating prices of local and imported goods. In villages in the Nile Province of Uganda, Akenda-Ondoga (1980) found that the high proportion of young household heads indicated a reversal of the southward flow of young male migrants to sugar plantations, where wages were too low and the costs of living were too high. Households hired-in little labour, nor were they suppliers of labour migrants.

An account of a post-migration economy is given by Pottier (1983), who investigated a set of Mambwe villages in northern Zambia. This area in the 1950s was a classic labour reserve of circulatory migrants who went into the copper belt, but the decline in copper mining and the limited opportunities in the urban 'informal' sector has disrupted the pattern of labour migration. Over the years, the

Mambwe have become dependent on imported consumer goods provided by wage labour, and since little was invested in improving agriculture in their home area either by the government or themselves, they have turned to other sources of income. They have filled a niche as local traders and contraband traders, which has been possible due to the decay in the distribution systems related to the collapse of government co-operatives, the scarcity of imported goods related to the vagaries of the world copper market, and the disruption of the transport system due to the conflict in Zimbabwe, which was only partially resolved by the re-opening of the railway in 1978. Apart from some improvement in bean-farming for the line-of-rail markets, farming has deteriorated, as the Mambwe have not returned to the land, and cassava, which needs lower labour inputs, has spread at the expense of millet, although nutritionally it is less acceptable.

SUMMARY

This chapter has looked at the ways in which labour is hired by African farmers as they have become more and more involved in the market economy. Hired workers are used by peasant farmers on a short-term basis to overcome seasonal, or temporary, bottlenecks in the labour supply, especially when commercial crops comprise a substantial proportion of their farming activities. But there are also increasing numbers of 'semi-capitalist' farmers in commercial-crop zones who rely heavily on hired workers. Also the growth of capitalist relations of production can be quite advanced in the peripheries of large towns, where the use of hired farm labour is widespread. As the pressure on land for farming and building increases on the edges of towns, the number of landless or land-poor peasants rises, who then become 'semi-proletarians'. Equally many farmers enter the urban industrial and commercial sectors as the income from trading or wage employment is either better than, or supplements that derived from farming. 'Proletarianization' is a complex process in rural Africa and the retention of rights to land frequently puts off the severance of many workers from their means of production, and proletarianization is neither complete nor irreversible.

Farm labour can be mobilized locally, regionally or internationally and the redistribution of labour gives rise to high levels of mobility. Labour is hired on a variety of contractual terms, which are very flexible and may be part of the transition to the establishment of a permanent wage labour force. From the nineteenth century onwards, the production of agricultural surpluses has been dependent on labour from economically-underdeveloped areas in order to supplement local supplies, which are limited by low population levels. But alternative sources of non-domestic labour were also available through the use of labour co-operation either for the production of food staples or commercial crops. As slavery decayed these communal groups played an important part in the development of small-commodity production, although they have declined in recent times, or more importantly been transformed into hired gang labour used by capitalist farmers. Any account of African farming would be incomplete without a discussion of labour-exchange systems and work groups, and the next chapter looks at methods of organizing farm labour through co-operation between domestic groups, rather than within them.

5

LABOUR CO-OPERATION: GROWTH, DECLINE AND PERSISTENCE

Labour co-operation is based on principles which extend beyond family and kinship, and is the means whereby massive inputs of labour can be mobilized within the rural community. Labour co-operation can be particularly important where farming practices demand short bursts of heavy work, such as clearing forest and bush, which lie beyond the capability of domestic groups, at least if they are to be accomplished in good time. Also, group labour can exist when the market for hired labour is undeveloped or shallow, and where job opportunities are limited and landlessness is not a major problem. Certain types of labour co-operation are the antithesis of 'proletarianization' and may limit or deflect the growth of economic differences within a community; therefore, the persistence or decay of communal labour may serve as an indicator of the penetration of rural societies by the market economy, and of capitalist farming. This chapter looks at the development and decay of work groups, and how they have undergone adaptation and change as production for the market and individualization have become characteristic of the rural economy.

FORMS OF LABOUR CO-OPERATION

The definition of co-operative labour is not easy, as it appears in many forms and is covered by terms such as reciprocal labour, labour exchange, festive work parties, beer parties and collective labour. We might begin by saying that it is an arrangement whereby members of a rural community join together to perform a task, or series of tasks, for a beneficiary whose relationship with the group is other than that of employer to employee (Moore, 1975). Another approach is to see how a number of people combine to perform specific tasks, such as clearing or weeding, which is the responsibility of an individual, yet is being done by a group. It is also possible to look at the size of groups, methods of recruitment, their structure and the type of jobs done. There are plenty of ways of categorizing co-operative labour, but we shall follow Moore's proposal that labour groups can be divided into two basic categories (Moore, 1975). These two categories are *exchange labour* and *festive labour*; in the later part of this chapter we shall discuss hired gang labour which is a modern adaptation of traditional forms of labour co-operation.

The difference between exchange labour and festive labour lies in the degree of reciprocity; indeed, the extent to which groups are reciprocal or non-reciprocal is a basic issue in the discussion of co-operative labour. Exchange labour usually involves a small number of households – rarely above ten – who combine on a basis of strict reciprocity, although the measurement of work done varies from days and hours to agreed amounts of land worked. The work may comprise variable amounts of all farm activities, and there is no payment to group members except a standard meal, or meals. Exchange labour may be between individuals, or among a group of farmers, but their size is limited because of the increased complexity of organizing large numbers of people when strict reciprocity has to be observed. For example, in the Gambia where the cultivation of swamp rice is particularly labour-intensive, the women from several compounds join together to weed each other's farms in turn, irrespective of the size of their plots, which usually means small groups of five to seven women. Exchange labour of this kind was used by 12 per cent of all farming households observed in one village, but a greater proportion – 30 per cent – used this type of labour for weeding groundnuts. Furthermore, these groups were based on close bonds between compounds, either of kinship, or affinal ties, but in some cases close friends would combine their labour (Haswell, 1953).

According to Seibel and Massing (1974), in Liberia workgroups formed on a reciprocal basis are very important in the western half of the country where the bulk of the work on upland rice farms is done in this manner; the incidence of reciprocal workgroups is less in the eastern half of the country and they are much smaller in size. The workgroups in the west of Liberia are unusual in that they can number up to thirty persons, requiring officers, rules and set methods of working which demand a high level of organization. In this area, population densities are low and the bush-fallowing of upland rice demands short but intensive bursts of energy. Participant farmers stated that these workgroups were the means of getting jobs done faster and in a more congenial manner. These Liberian workgroups are divided into a men's group doing the heavier work in the first part of the cultivation cycle – brushing, felling and burning – while in the second half of the cycle women's groups predominated for weeding and harvesting.

The other principal type of labour co-operation is through what is known as festive labour, which in East Africa is frequently referred to as 'beer parties'. Festive labour is organized on an *ad hoc* basis for specific tasks and the rewards for work in drinks and food can be quite lavish, depending on the status of the host. Kinship and clientage may be the basis of their formation, but reciprocity is poorly-developed and may only apply to the host's kin giving their labour, rather than himself. Festive work parties are large and the rewards for work are immediate rather than delayed, as in the case of labour exchange groups. According to Mayer's account of festive workgroups among the Gussii of Kenya, the group (*risaga*) is permanent in the sense it lasts throughout the farming year and is territorial, involving up to fifty adults, with possible subdivisions into smaller groups of seven to ten adults (Mayer, 1951). The groups are formed on the basis of bonds between neighbours and their economic interdependence, and although kinship may reinforce these qualities it is not essential to their foundation. The territorial nature of groups reflects the dispersal of settlement among the Gussii, and the needs of neighbouring compounds to pool their labour resources, especially for heavy tasks such as clearing land. The *risaga* is also used when outside help is needed due to illness, the miscalculation of weather signs, or simply inefficiency. The groups lack formal authority and leadership, which Mayer believed to be a function of Gussii institutions and their lack of centralized authority. Similar conditions apply to festive workgroups in the Gambia among the sedentary Fulani and the Mandinka, where festive workgroups are spontaneous, with no formalized structure. The prospective host tells friends he needs workers on a particular day, and friends bring other friends, and the group develops according to the size of the field and the host's capacity to provide food, drinks and kola. As in the case of the Gussii, anyone can call a festive group, provided he has the means to give sufficient food or, in the case of the Gussii, beer. Mayer noted that there was a tendency for the wealthier households to call them more frequently, while poorer ones called smaller and more localized *risaga*, using women, who were paid only in food, usually bananas.

Festive workgroups are widespread throughout tropical Africa and although they have undergone a relative decline compared with labour exchange groups, they may well form the basis of contemporary hired gang labour, inasmuch as their lack of reciprocity is a means of transferring labour from poorer farmers to 'big-men' and emergent capitalist farmers. It is apparent that exchange labour groups and festive workgroups differ not only in their organization, but support different production relationships, especially at either end of the continuum of reciprocity and non-reciprocity. Among labour exchange groups there is a tendency for the participants to be approximately of the same social and economic status, and they may help to slow the development of hired wage labour, or at least to keep the price down. On the other hand as we have noted, festive workgroups may be used to transfer labour services to wealthier members of the community such as traders, larger farmers and also to political and religious leaders, and more recently leaders of modern political parties.

Obligatory social labour is commonplace in rural areas, and, for example, in the Gambia the headman of the village may have one field weeded by the women of the village, who do this in recognition of his duties performed for the benefit of the community, which prevents him carrying out some of his farmwork. Likewise the head musician and praise-singer receive labour services from the community. A more widespread social obligation is the provision by young men of farmwork for future fathers-in-law. Alternatively, married women in some patri-local societies, such as the Mandinka, may still return to their fathers' farms to give labour services after they have married, usually to help with harvesting (Pélissier, 1966). As we have observed before, marriage and affinal ties may produce intricate patterns in the deployment of farm labour.

Festive work parties may evolve into capitalist forms of labour, and arguably social obligation may become the means of extracting surpluses from poorer farmers to the detriment of their own farms, by reducing the time they spend on them. This is especially the case when the traditional festive workgroup becomes more permanent and increasingly used by elders and 'big-men', taking advantage of the growth of external markets for cash crops, and using labour groups to reach these markets. But this forms the theme of our discussion in the last part of this chapter.

Another type of labour group, which is marginally different from the two we have discussed so far, is that based upon age-sets. In its purest form it is usually a cohort whose membership is defined ritually by initiation ceremonies. The membership criteria are constant, but the type of work undertaken varies, as well as the beneficiaries. Age may be used to define the membership of labour exchange groups, and may be the means whereby young men perform the work to be done for 'bride-service' as part of marriage contracts. Age-setting may also be the means whereby the community gets certain projects completed such as wells dug, or mosques built. On the other hand they have been construed as the means of transferring the labour surplus of the young to the elders, especially in those societies where age and sex are important parameters of differentiation (Meillasoux, 1972). It may be that it is this type of exploitation which has led to the decline of age-sets, as young men use external job opportunities to limit their dependence on elders.

THE ECONOMIC BENEFITS OF LABOUR GROUPS

The benefits of labour groups are numerous, but we shall consider primarily those that relate to economic advantages. As we pointed out in Chapter 1, arduousness and urgency figure significantly in the work-cycle of peasant farmers, and the speed with which a job can be completed and its correct timing can materially affect yields and the difference between sufficient and insufficient food supplies. If we add illness and sudden death to the fluctuating demands of the production process, then flexibility in the face of uncertainty becomes paramount. Under these conditions, co-operative labour can become an essential ingredient in farming systems, especially where there is either no landless proletariat, or a limited one. Co-operative labour groups allow the use of irregular labour inputs, often on a massive scale, which means that delays in the farming cycle can be made good. Even if wage labour is available, and even if it is cheaper than feeding a workgroup, the availability may be limited and, as Mayer (1951) observed in his work on the Gussii, no farmer could guarantee that he could go out into his own or a neighbouring community and pick up fifteen to thirty workers on a particular day. Where the labour market is imperfectly developed, the use of either labour exchange or other institutionalized means of labour recruitment serves an important function.

The economies of scale encourage the use of workgroups, and large festive work parties are often used in rotational bush-fallow systems where clearing involves heavy work. Swampland-rice cultivation also demands heavy and continuous work for the preparation of seed-beds, bunding, transplanting and harvesting rice. In Senegal and the Gambia, rice farming is often done by women, and labour exchange groups are used which are internally differentiated by age; the younger women (25–30 years) who are physically strong are complemented by older, weaker women who are knowledgeable and skilled in rice techniques (Weil, 1978). Other reasons for the combination of neighbours or kin include the advantage of those with adjacent fields joining together to carry out the simple, but time-consuming, job of shifting predators, such as rats. The participants of workgroups often believe that the advantages are social or psychological, and that work done jointly is less tedious and pleasanter. Tasks such as weeding or harvesting, if not arduous, are prolonged, and the use of music and song are commonplace in the performance of agricultural jobs.

But the use of co-operative labour has particular advantages in two areas, which are in part interrelated: the introduction of new crops and techniques, and the problem of cash-flow. Co-operative workgroups are commonly applied to those parts of the farming cycle where bottlenecks in the labour supply occur, which may be exacerbated by the introduction of ploughing, either using oxen, or hiring-in tractor-ploughs. The large areas cultivated through ploughing tend to push the demand for labour further along the sequence of operations, so that more labour is required for weeding and harvesting of the increased area cultivated. Similarly, as we have seen, the introduction of new crops may overlap, or directly conflict, with food staples, and raises the demand for labour which cannot be met from within the domestic group. An added advantage of communal labour (and not only for 'big-men' farmers) is that they avoid the need for cash payments. On the one hand, in economies which have undergone relatively little commoditization, hired labour is a very limited option; on the other hand, when cash crops are introduced it still may be inconvenient, or unlikely, that enough surplus cash is held over from the previous season to pay labourers, and credit facilities (other than money-lenders) are not available for small farmers. Reciprocal labour exchanges are a way out of labour bottlenecks for small farmers, while bigger farmers may accumulate surplus food, if not cash, to use for large festive work parties.

Although labour co-operation is an important aspect of farming, yet little is known about its origins or role in agricultural change. For example, to what extent was the cash-crop revolution of the nineteenth to early twentieth centuries dependent upon the use of co-operative labour groups, at least in the formative years of cash crop production, if not at a later stage when hired labour was more available and accessible for a larger sector of the rural community? Mayer's work among the Gussii of Kenya was being done at the time when ploughing and cash cropping were beginning to change the Gussii economy, and although ploughing was not in itself suited to the use of *risaga*, nonetheless, as his informants said, the more one ploughs, the more one calls! Likewise the avoidance of cash payments was much in evidence.

On the question of costs, Mayer found that *risaga* labour was in fact slightly cheaper than hired labour, although it has been contended that co-operative labour groups have become dearer, as the price of food and drink has risen. But in 1948 the 'cost' of grain for beer for a four-hour stint worked out at 1/12th of a shilling per man hour compared with 1/10th of a shilling for hired labour. Furthermore *risaga* labour was considered to work harder (an assertion which conflicts with other accounts). Putting efficiency, hard work and cost to one side, there is still the advantage that co-operative labour provided concentrated effort at a particular moment in time. Marginal calculations are in one sense not relevant under these conditions, and even if one has to take thirty workers when twenty-five would do, the advantage of access, payment in kind and immediacy can be paramount. No doubt co-operative labour helps to keep down the development and cost of hired labour, yet the access to festive work parties by the more influential and wealthy in the community is a means of transferring labour surpluses and building up a rural capitalist sector. Co-operative labour may well have been influential in the success of commercial agriculture, and at a cost born not by the emergent class of capitalist farmers, but by poorer members of the community.

The advantages of co-operative labour are more apparent in the cultivation of certain crops and in the techniques employed, but in many parts of tropical Africa where population densities are low, the best way for poorer farmers to mobilize large amounts of non-domestic labour lies in exchange workgroups. The absence of a landless labour force and limited arrangements for borrowing money, other than at exorbitant rates, means that workgroups can be an alternative to hired labour. A limiting factor may be the extent to which a community has been depleted by out-migration of younger men, who form the core of workgroups. Labour co-operation can be viewed as a transitional form between non-capitalist relations of production and the parallel with share-contracts is apparent. Share-contracts have been seen as a link between forms of production which relied heavily on slave labour and more capitalist forms using hired labour; co-operative workgroups may occupy a similar role and it is appropriate for us to pay some attention to the notion that they may have been of particular importance after the decline of slavery. The share-contract has been generally accepted as the means whereby commercial cropping, at least in its initial stages, was given a considerable boost; a similar role for co-operative labour seems to have been ignored.

THE DEVELOPMENT OF CO-OPERATIVE LABOUR AND THE DECLINE OF SLAVERY

Until the end of the nineteenth century there were many parts of tropical Africa where slavery was an integral part of the economy; thereafter slavery began to decay, assisted by the abolitionist measures of the colonialists, as well as by general structural changes in the African economy under colonialism. Slaves formed a significant part of pre-colonial societies among the Maraka (of the middle Niger Valley), the Yoruba and the Asante, and in the Sokoto Caliphate, the Sudan, Biafra and along the East African coast; estimates suggest that between one-quarter and one-half of the population were slaves (Lovejoy, 1981). Slavery was a major means of organizing labour for diverse purposes such as mining, porterage and domestic farming. The nature of slavery is complex, but basically it was a specific form of exploitation which ultimately rested on coercion, regarding slaves as a form of property. However, it is necessary to make a distinction between the status and condition of slaves; their status may have been clear, but their condition varied and there were slaves who were materially well-off and who held important offices in pre-colonial states. Lovejoy (1981) has suggested that slavery must be seen in the context of the ideology which legitimates it, while accepting that the actual economic and social circumstances of slavery often differed from its ideology; in other words, there was a divergence between theory and practice. Under Islam, slavery was a means of conversion and indoctrination of non-believers, but economically slaves were a vital source of labour and of soldiers. Under kinship idioms, slaves were defined as non-kin, but they could be slowly assimilated and slave-women were an ideal source of additional wives, who were valuable economic assets not only as workers but as producers of more producers.

Although slavery may be capable of different definitions and assumed diverse forms, slaves were not simply a means of extended prestige through larger kinship groups; they were economic assets in societies where power and influence was vested in those who had control over manpower. Slaves were used by chiefs and rulers in mines and agricultural work and they served as porters; but they also were used at the domestic level, where they worked alongside the sons of their owners. We have already discussed the form of domestic organization in Nigeria called *gandu* (pl. *gandaye*) which in its most complete form comprised not only fathers and married sons, but also slaves and their dependants. All adult male slaves had their own farms which they worked at agreed times; in some cases the division of time was so many days per week, or alternatively set periods during each working day. The food given to slaves from the common granary was related to these work periods; otherwise they provided their own means of subsistence from their own plots; and partially reproduced their households. Similar patterns of shared time existed in the middle Niger Valley, Senegal, the Gambia and Sierra Leone. However, slaves on plantations probably fared less well in terms of land and shared time.

The introduction of commercial crops in the nineteenth century, as we have seen, intensified agricultural labour, and in the initial phases of commercial cultivation the labour provided by slaves was far from negligible. As the Atlantic slave trade disappeared the development of legitimate trade and the penetration of European merchant capital stimulated the use of slaves for the production of commercial crops. For example, in Senegal and the Gambia in the mid nineteenth century the groundnut trade relied heavily on slaves and migrant labour (Swindell, 1980), while palm-oil in Yorubaland was initiated by big-men with large labour forces made up of kinsmen and slaves (Clarke, 1981). In East Africa slaves were used in the clove industry (Cooper, 1982), while in Zaire slavery only became widespread in the nineteenth century as the region became part of the world trading economy (Jewsiewicki and Bawele, 1982).

The decay of slavery in the early twentieth century occurred by means of defection (see Roberts and Klein, 1980) and through abolition; the resulting changes in the relations of production were not lost either on the colonial authorities, or on those they ruled. Abolition was something of a gradualist measure as colonial officers were aware of the possible disruption it might cause, especially where export crops were already established. On the other hand they were also aware that the mobilization of the labour required by the towns, transport systems and commercial-crop regions needed a more flexible system, in which migrant labour and labour resources would have to play a part. As we have seen crops such as cocoa, coffee, cotton and groundnuts have seasonally-determined labour requirements; the decay and abolition of slavery released a hitherto immobilized labour force which was used in the development of commercial cropping.

If former slaves set up independent farming households, then their former owners could be faced with a reduced labour supply while their access to land remained undisturbed. Therefore, if former owners wished to keep their farms fully operational, they had to retain a client relationship with their former slaves, or resort to hired labour. The evidence about the defection of slaves and their transformation into independent farmers is contradictory, and suggests that there were regional variations. Hill (1976) has argued that in Hausaland there was a relatively easy shift from slave to freeman farmer, but Smith (1955) believed that clientage persisted, and slaves and their descendants often stayed with their owners after abolition. The element of clientage and kinship is present in some forms of co-operative labour, and the use of festive workgroups in particular may have been the answer to reduced labour forces, especially for those with large farms who formerly had numerous slaves.

Co-operative labour may be a relatively recent phenomenon, or at least one which became more widespread and important after the decline of domestic slavery and the development of new cropping systems. Extra labour was needed both by former slaves and their owners as domestic units began to show signs of a decrease in size, at the same time as new crops and markets were being developed. Even if labour co-operation was not entirely a post-abolition phenomenon, then its use may have become more pressing in the initial stages of commercial crop production and commoditization of the economy. The use of labour co-operation, especially festive workgroups by village heads, religious functionaries and emergent capitalist farmers, looks suspiciously like the acquisition of large labour forces which had previously been available through the ownership of slaves. Also, many freemen farmers who would not wish to hire themselves out locally to former slaves, may have had no qualms about joining in local workgroups, on either an exchange or a non-exchange basis.

PERSISTENCE OR DECLINE? THE PRESENT STATE OF LABOUR CO-OPERATION

The origins of co-operative labour may have received relatively scant attention, but there has been plenty of discussion about its decline. When looking at the decline of co-operative labour, one may have to be careful about self-interested accounts by older members of a community who continually mourn the passing of a form of labour organization from which they have most to gain. But allowing for a measure of caution, there are numerous accounts which indicate a decline rather than persistence. Uchendu (1970) lists a variety of causes: technical progress, monetization of the economy, increased specialization of tasks, the high cost of feeding festive work parties, the breakdown of traditional sanctions needed to organize and control workgroups, and the emergence of a rural proletariat. Erasmus (1956), who examined workgroups in South America, adds to this list of causes the poor quality of much communal work, and the development of the *mores* of individualism. Individualism includes both the impersonal relationships of hiring strangers, and conspicuous consumption (especially of non-local goods) as a means of social approbation rather than calling large workgroups.

We have already suggested that some reasons for decline need to be qualified; for example, technical progress and the introduction of cash crops may not always lead to a decline, although there may be a shift from festive workgroups to labour exchange. The argument about the decline of cooperative labour may best be approached by looking at different types of social and economic change, in order to analyse the present and future state of labour co-operation, in particular by considering three major factors or situations: population growth, the emergence of a landless labour force, and increased monetization of the economy. A fourth is the introduction of full-time non-farm employment (Moore, 1975).

In the first instance population growth may take place where there is no significant change in land distribution and tenure. The rise in population may alter the land-surplus economy, which can lead to a decline in the use of co-operative labour. This assumes that units of land farmed become smaller and are more intensively cultivated, obviating the need for co-operation. Also, if there is an increase in labour- and skill-intensive jobs, such as occurs in a move from more extensive to intensive forms of agriculture, then the quality of work has to be better, and this may gradually rule out the use of festive workgroups, while still encouraging the use of small labour-exchange groups approximating to strict reciprocity. The move from extensive upland-rice farming to intensive paddy-rice farming is a case in point. Plots are smaller, seedbeds have to be made, transplanting is time-consuming and needs some care. Increased frequency of cropping is another change in practice which is likely to reduce the formation and use of *ad hoc* festive work parties. The argument about population and man–land ratios is of course incomplete without considering the size of domestic production units themselves. The decline in the size of production units may well reduce the number of participants available for exchange labour (for example, young men) but it may well increase the need for it. The author's own work in the Gambia showed that farming households comprising a man, his wives and unmarried sons used non-family labour as part of their farming strategies, especially when groundnuts were integrated with food crops. Also, within small family production units the dynamics of the family life-cycle affect them to a much greater degree than extended lineage groupings; when the children are young, the dependency ratio of active to non- or partially-active members increases. When small family production units develop in areas of low population density, the need for co-operation continues, whereas in areas of high population density a decrease in the size of production units may be overcome if smaller plots and more intensive methods obtain.

As the rural community becomes differentiated into richer and poorer farmers, net transfers of labour may occur in favour of the former, which means an increase in their supervisory function and a diminution of their role as farm workers. Thus the richer farmer, who has more land, may no longer wish to take part in labour groups, especially on an exchange basis, as the returns are less than if he remains a supervisor of his farms and his workers. If there are no landless labourers, the richer farmer may employ festive labour if it is an effective means of appropriating the labour of poorer farmers who still have access to land. But under conditions of increasing population density and commoditization, a class of landless or land-poor farmers may emerge, together with farmers who are only partially occupied; then the chances are that they will work for wages lower than the costs of providing refreshment for festive work parties, and submit to labour discipline. Under these circumstances wage labour begins to replace festive labour. An additional attraction for the richer farmer is that he can apply marginal units of labour, rather than taking work parties on a 'come-one-come-all' basis.

For poorer farmers, the use of wage labour is difficult to predict, and a crucial factor is cash availability and the unorganized state of the labour markets. In these circumstances exchange groups will tend to persist, especially if poorer farmers have to compete with the richer ones for the limited supply of hired wage labour. The use of shared time (like shared crops) may be an intermediate phase in the development of hired labour, especially among small-commodity producers, and its persistence depends on local conditions. But as the development of wage labour and capitalist relations allows farmers themselves to enter into the non-agricultural economy as part-time labourers, it reduces the prospect of domestic groups fulfilling their obligations to communal labour groups.

Much of the evidence points to a decline in labour cooperation with festive workgroups being the most affected. Festive groups may be less efficient and wage labour soon replaces them as a means of extracting surpluses by bigger farmers. But it would seem that exchange labour, based on small numbers and approximating to strict reciprocity, offers a good deal to smaller farmers who still have access to sufficient land. Furthermore, if these farmers have limited access to non-farm work opportunities, and they cultivate crops such as rice, cotton or groundnuts, with high seasonal labour peaks, then exchange labour persists.

But persistence and decline are not the only possibilities we need to discuss; it is appropriate at the end of this discussion to look at how labour groups have developed into hired gang labour, which has been associated with the growth of capitalist farming. Strictly speaking, hired gang labour is not the same as labour co-operation; but there seems little doubt that it has evolved from festive workgroups and fulfils the function of transferring labour surpluses from smaller to bigger farmers in the community. An intermediate form of hired gang labour is where a group may use the money as a means of raising credit for members, or of raising capital for communal works, or for religious organizations. In other words they are *corporate* wage earning organizations, rather than a means of providing *individual* wages for members by sharing the proceeds of the workgroup fees. Examples from the Gambia and Kenya can be used to demonstrate the contemporary use of hired group labour, how it is organized, and who are the beneficiaries.

In the Upper River area of the Gambia Wedderburn (1977) recognized three types of labour organization: festive work parties, group or individual exchange labour, and what he refers to as 'organized work parties'. The latter comprised permanent or semi-permanent structures with elected officers, rules of procedure and fines for non-attendance; and, unlike festive or exchange labour, they hired themselves out for cash. Primarily they were used by other farmers for weeding, and their composition was varied according to sex, age and their particular objectives in working together. For example, in the village of Mansajang, which had in 1976 a population of around 750, the largest organized workgroup comprised some ninety women, both married and unmarried. Originally there was one larger women's festive workgroup covering the whole village, which later split into two; one half became an organized workgroup, the other half remained as it was; significantly the new group was called out ten times in the season, while the festive work party was called out on only two occasions. In Mansajang hired labour was not the preferred type; either migrants who came on a shared-time and land basis

(Strange Farmers) or paid workgroups were more popular. The women's workgroup, although totalling ninety women, varied in size throughout the working day to allow women to integrate domestic chores, and a maximum of forty to fifty were at work at any one time. The standard charge per day was 30 *dalasi* (£7.50), which was irrespective of field or job size; failure to attend once the group was called led to a fine of one *dalasi* (£0.25). The group worked only on Fridays and was chiefly hired to work on rice and groundnut farms.

The proceeds of a season's work by this workgroup were used for social purposes, but more importantly served as a credit fund for the members, to assist them with their own farms. In the village there also existed other forms of paid-labour groups. Small workgroups of male teenagers were formed comprising six or thirty members working for 10 *dalasi* (£2.50) per half-day; the proceeds were used for social purposes, such as sports clubs. Also there were groups of a dozen or so boys aged about ten years who hired themselves out simply to accumulate pocket money. Finally, there were other young men who cultivated a communal groundnut farm the produce of which was loaned to members to provide seed nuts at 100 per cent interest; after a few years the total accumulated stock is sold to buy mechanical farm equipment for the use of members. Thus there were a number of hired workgroups in Mansajang whose objectives ranged from purely social, to various types of credit and saving organizations. But in terms of beneficiaries there was little doubt that prosperous farmers used them on most occasions, and this is supported by the author's own observations in the Gambia, where paid workgroups were employed by households who had members working in nearby towns, who replaced them by hiring-in workers and paying them from the proceeds of wages, salaries or profits from trading (Swindell, 1978). In Mansajang communal labour was used by large, medium and small families, but proportionately greater use (60 per cent of all labour groups) came from those households with the largest farms and access to other resources, such as surplus food.

According to Wedderburn (1977) the use of hired labour (both individual and paid workgroups) has developed since 1969, as more members of farming households have engaged in non-farm activities. Mansajang is a village close to the largest up-river town of Basse, which offers a range of off-farm employment and reflects the importance of the location of rural communities in determining the amount and rates of change in such things as workgroups and hired labour. For example, in Sierra Leone semi-capitalist farmers in the urban periphery hire gang labour from the town and arrange for them to be transported out to the farms daily (Binns, 1981). Wedderburn suggests that festive workgroups were formerly much larger and drawn from neighbouring villages as well as from within Mansajang; such extra-village workgroups were called by 'big-men' anxious to establish their prestige, as well as larger farms, usually for commercial groundnut farming. The use of festive work parties declined as members began to measure the opportunity cost of their labour not in terms of work foregone on their own farms, but of missed chances of wage-paid work in the village or nearby town. Although labour exchange groups are still used in Mansajang, the core of 'traditional' labour co-operation lies in the days of obligatory labour given to village heads, religious functionaries and kinsmen. Parallel to these traditional forms of communal labour is the growth of paid gang labour which has developed as part of the increased economic differentiation within the community and its integration into the market economy.

Hired-labour groups assume a variety of functions in Mansajang and show a good deal of flexibility and adaptation. It would seem that similar developments can be found in many parts of tropical Africa and, for example, Charsley (1976) has studied labour groups in Uganda which are both recent and adaptive. In fact Charsley challenges the assumption that workgroups should be categorized as 'traditional', uneconomic, and barriers to progress and therefore part of a vanishing order. Such 'modernization' perspectives may be unsound (at least in the short term), as they are based on incorrect premises about the immediate future of rural communities. Charsley was interested in groups of Kenyans who established themselves in western Uganda in the 1950s as farmers on agricultural settlement schemes. Known locally as Maragoli, these people cultivated 23-acre plots growing maize as a food staple and selling any surpluses, together with cotton, their principal cash crop. Settlement farmers hired labourers, some of whom came as migrants from Rwanda, but they also had access to machinery from the tractor-hire units. The Maragoli were in no way isolated from the market economy, nor from technical innovation, yet communal labour groups flourished alongside hired and domestic labour.

The work groups which Charsley studied were known as *silika* (pl. *tsisilika*) and were recruited either on a clan basis or from Christian congregations. The Maragoli are characterized by a large number of small religious groups of great denominational diversity. In the study area in 1968 Charsley found some seventeen denominations and thirty-two congregations, which commonly comprised between eleven and twenty adults. Congregations proved the most stable basis for recruiting communal labour groups, which met under the control of the leader of the congregation on two or three days per week. Land clearing and weeding were the most frequent tasks undertaken, and the host provided tea, food and a fee for church funds. The costs of *silika* labour seemed relatively low, 1.00–2.00 shillings per person per day, compared with 2.00 shillings plus food for hired labour; the quality of work done was good but the quantity in terms of area covered was less than for hired labour.

Although reciprocity operates in the *silika* system it cannot be on a strictly one-to-one basis, as workloads and farm sizes are not equal. Also some congregational members who were household heads considered the opportunity costs of *silika* work and sent wives and sons, as they themselves had jobs elsewhere. It appeared that 40 per cent of the Maragoli did not participate, notably the larger farmers and emergent rural capitalists on the one hand, and the ne'er-do-wells on the other. The *silika* embraced the 'good and the average', whereas the hirers were only peripherally involved. The *silika* exists in Kenya, but is largely run by women, probably because of extensive out-migration by males; in its Christian male-dominated form in Uganda it appears to be an adaptation by migrants. As economic differentiation has developed among the Maragoli, so the reciprocal arrangements have tended to break down, but a body of potential participants, especially medium-scale peasant farmers, may well persist for some time, and in the early days of Maragoli settlement in Uganda, the *silika* may have underpinned their economic survival.

SUMMARY

Exchange labour and festive labour groups are widespread in tropical Africa and show not only indications of persistence and decline, but of adaptation to meet new economic circumstances. Communal labour appears to work well in areas of low population density especially if bush-fallowing is practised and economic differentiation is limited. Economic differentiation may be softened or delayed by communal labour, although in the case of festive workgroups the more influential often benefit most and appropriate surplus labour from the other households; once economic differentiation gains ground, then work groups may decline or be adapted and become the core of hired-labour gangs. Labour exchanges conducted on a reciprocal basis among a small number of farmers seem to persist, as they have advantages for medium-sized households who lack the necessary money capital to pay wages.

Communal labour is often held up as an example of corporate interest and endeavour and as part of traditional African society and values. However, the origins of communal labour are obscure and there is every reason to suppose that they are relatively recent and were given a great boost with the decline of domestic slavery and agrestic servitude, just at the time when labour was needed to promote the expansion of commercial crops. The role of communal labour in the early stages of commercial agriculture for the export market remains unexplored, and possibly underestimated. Communal labour may have been an important innovation in the transition from societies where either slaves, or extended kinship groups, were important sources of surplus labour, to a situation where smaller domestic groups involved in commodity production needed extra supplies, but were unable either to 'purchase' or recruit it where labour markets were shallow.

Whatever the origins and nature of labour co-operation may be, it has not stopped it being utilized as an example of traditional African life by development planners seeking to improve contemporary farming. This has been the case in countries such as Tanzania which have made serious attempts to introduce socialist programmes of rural change aimed at limiting the development of a petty-bourgeoisie. Such attempts have met with limited success, but this is part and parcel of the general issue of labour relations between peasants and state bureaucracies to which we turn next.

6

FARM LABOUR AND PROGRAMMES OF AGRARIAN CHANGE

The peasant may have been the 'hero' of the African cash-crop revolution, but he has become the universal 'villain' in the scenarios of modernization and economic development. Induced changes in peasant and small-commodity production were first attempted by the colonial authorities and then by post-colonial states using various forms of intervention and control. Agricultural resettlement schemes, mechanization programmes, irrigation, co-operatives, integrated development projects and extension schemes have met with responses ranging from partial acceptance, through indifference to outright resistance. Agrarian State capitalism as well as the socialist transformation of rural communities has sustained some spectacular reversals as the peasant remains 'uncaptured' by the modern state. Anger, despair and cynicism are not uncommon among politicians, bureaucrats and aid-managers, and there is no shortage of explanations as to why peasants are reluctant to be integrated into the national economies and to become more 'efficient' producers.

Interest in peasant resistance has grown among academic researchers, although, for reasons referred to later, there has been less interest among politicians and bureaucrats. Explanations of failure frequently rest upon peasant stupidity, illiteracy, and administrative shortcomings, as well as an imperfect understanding of environmental constraints.

Problems of implementation, poor administrative infrastructures and personnel do play a part, but it is necessary to go beyond these more obvious shortcomings and inquire about who is resisting whom, and whose interests programmes of agricultural transformation actually serve (Cohen and Hutton, 1975).

Ostensibly all schemes of economic change and improvement set out to serve the interest of the majority of peasant farmers, but in reality they proceed from a desperate need of African States to extract surpluses and revenues to finance their growing expenditures. Yet the problem is that the bulk of production is decentralized and remains in the hands of small-scale farmers, petty-traders and business men. Also, peasant farmers do not perceive the advantage of complying with schemes which incorporate them into national objectives and markets from which experience tells them they have little to gain. The penetration of agricultural production by State capital can lead to increased economic differentiation and, like many 'green revolutions', can work in the favour of the already better-off farmers or urban entrepreneurs, rather than of the bulk of the peasantry, for whose interests the schemes are supposedly designed. It is arguable that induced structural change by the intervention of State capital can never be equitable, and that development and equality are not viable options. Yet the polarization and differentials they engender may be the necessary prelude to more effective change arising from a clash of group or class interests. Where radical change through State farms and collectivization has been attempted specifically to promote conditions of equality, the problem has been the fervour with which peasants have stuck to their private plots and the surpluses they produce.

Two root problems of African rural development appear to be the continuing access of peasants to farmland through traditional systems of use-right, and labour-intensive farming systems and the productive relationships which characterize them. This is not the place to enter into an extended discussion of rival theories of economic development and change, nor to analyse the shortcomings and failures of various schemes. But it is necessary to look at the role of farm labour in programmes of agricultural transformation and improvement, and how farmers have reacted to, and coped with induced change. It is also necessary to consider whether the schemes have misunderstood the nature of the production process and the relations of production, so that resistance is almost inevitable. It is for these reasons that arguments about relations of production, economic differentiation, peasants and small-commodity producers, and migrant labour are not just academic issues, but have a direct relevance to the restructuring of rural communities and national programmes of economic survival and development.

This chapter begins by looking at some of the reasons for State intervention in agriculture and what motivates continued attempts to transform agriculture, given the history of reversals recorded in just about every part of tropical Africa. The role of the modern State in Africa is an important contemporary issue and the incorporation of small-scale farmers into national economies is just as relevant as their incorporation into the world capitalist system. The less-than-complete shift to capitalist relations of production has attracted much attention, and as we mentioned earlier has led to diverse explanations, such as dependency theory, peripheral capitalism and the articulation of pre-capitalist modes of production. Less attention has been focussed on the dynamics within the 'periphery' and the aims and problems of implementing agrarian change by individual States. At the grass-roots level these national and international forces affect millions of peasant farmers and small-commodity producers, and in particular we explore how they may disrupt existing relations of production, or cause adaptation and the emergence of new patterns of farm labour.

STATE INTERVENTION

Large-scale agricultural development schemes financed by State capital began in the 1920s in the Sudan, where the British irrigated the area between the Blue Nile and the White Nile for the cultivation of cotton and sorghum. The French, equally anxious to secure supplies of cotton for their manufacturers, began similar irrigation schemes in the middle Niger and Senegal Valleys, also in the 1920s. Throughout the colonial period attempts were made to improve crop yields and cultivation techniques, especially of newly-introduced crops which were to be exported to the various *métropoles*. Schemes of improvement and transformation took many forms, but with the exception of the Gezira scheme in Sudan, large-scale agricultural technology has met with considerable resistance, although programmes of change aimed at the village level through forms of collectivization have fared little better. Why then do African States persist in their attempts to transform the agricultural sector, pursuing policies which have a history of failure, or limited success? As Hart (1982) observes, what appears parlous by standards of economic efficiency or public welfare is rational in the context of the institutional and material requirements of emergent states.

In the wake of Independence, modern African States were naturally keen to correct the shortcomings of colonial rule, and political and ideological goals were foremost in the minds of the cadres of graduates who formulated and administered policies, but their expectations frequently exceeded the revenues required. Colonial administrations had not been overly ambitious in the development of physical or administrative infrastructures, other than to facilitate the growth of exports, and the development of transport networks had been secured by using varying amounts of direct or indirect forced labour. Nor were government institutions often developed to serve advanced capitalist production, except in Kenya and the Rhodesias. Now all States have a pressing need for liquid resources to continue and expand their function, which means raising revenues from as wide a base as possible.

Both colonial and independent governments were faced with limited options for raising sufficient revenue; the taxation of peasant farmers and petty producers yields small returns, given the difficulties of administration, while direct taxes are useless. Import and export duties are frequently avoided by smugglers and border traders, and expatriate companies who are more amenable to taxation are often given 'tax-free holidays'. Under these conditions emergent States have had recourse to milking the funds of the co-operatives, seeking foreign aid and suppliers' credits, or floating their own currencies and financing the public debt by inflation and printing money. When these circumstances are set within the context of the terms of trade, increased food imports and rising world oil prices, the urge to intervene and transform the most basic sector of the economy, agriculture, is overwhelming. The aim of rural development schemes is not efficiency, but gross output, which at least yields some surplus and income for the State, even if overall agricultural performance is worse than peasant production (Hart, 1982).

The penetration of the rural sector by the State, whether it be done on broadly capitalist or socialist lines, is in order to secure control of production, which is dispersed among millions of small farmers, whose perception of the national economic interest is minimal. African farmers are not incapable of change, but development planning has had a limited impact on the rural sector; the reasons for this are numerous, but a crucial one for many producers is that schemes have little conception of how domestic groups organize and recruit labour, and how even with the best of wills they cannot meet the labour requirements of development programmes. Therefore, it is the supply and organization of farm labour in the context of development planning which is the chief issue in this concluding chapter, and one which brings to the fore the problem of resistance by peasant farmers and farm labour in the attempts made by the modern State to transform the most basic sector of its economy. Our discussion will be built around selected case studies of agrarian change, comprising West African rice schemes, irrigation projects in northern Nigeria and the *ujamaa* and villagization programmes in Tanzania.

WEST AFRICAN RICE SCHEMES

Rice cultivation is widespread throughout West Africa, although it becomes a major food staple only in the forest and Guinea savannahs westwards of the Ivory Coast, and is important along the coastal littoral. Basically there are two types of rice, upland and swamp rice. The former is grown on bush-farms using rotational-fallows to restore soil fertility; technology is limited to hoe and cutlass, with the seed sown in broadcast fashion. Swamp-rice cultivation is rather more varied and can be carried out on rain-fed swamps which are seasonally flooded, or in depressions where the water table rises in the wet season. Swamp rice can be sown broadcast, or in nurseries and then transplanted. Along rivers and coastal estuaries, grassland and mangrove can be cleared to reclaim land for freshwater or saltwater varieties of rice and under these conditions transplanting, or paddy-rice cultivation, is usually the norm. If swamps remain wet throughout the dry season, then rice may be double-cropped, or water control systems can be used, such as dams and bunding, to ensure at least two crops each year.

Although swamp-rice varieties were domesticated in the savannah river basins of West Africa thousands of years ago, the development of swamp cultivation and the introduction of new varieties date from the late nineteenth and early twentieth centuries. The natural diffusion of swamp cultivation which occurred along the coastal margins in the nineteenth century was given a determined push by the colonial authorities, a policy which has been continued by independent governments, and rice schemes of all shapes and sizes are an important element in development strategies in Senegal, the Gambia, Sierra Leone and Liberia. Rice has also become an important crop in development programmes in northern Ghana and in northern Nigeria.

There have been significant changes in food habits in West Africa during this century and governments have become seriously embarrassed by the rising levels of imported rice and wheat. The potential for wheat production is limited to the northern margins of the savannahs, but rice has a much bigger potential and the areas of 'unused' grassland and mangrove swamp and river floodland have an enormous attraction for governments looking for alternative food supplies. Furthermore, swamp rice can, under favourable conditions, produce over twice the yield per hectare of upland rice. But the fascination with land potential *per se* and a concentration on sets of 'land units', rather than sets of 'land users', has led to some unexpected outcomes.

Because much swampland was unused and unclaimed, it offered the chance of introducing mechanical cultivation, and tractor stations were set up by the British in all their West African territories, but with a special emphasis on Sierra Leone, where the swamp-rice potential appeared greatest. It had been estimated that some 500,000 acres of mangrove and grass swamps were available for cultivation, some of which were cultivated in the north on a limited scale before colonial rule. In 1947 a concerted effort was made to introduce the mechanical ploughing and harrowing of swamps cleared by farmers in the areas zoned for rice farming. The usual problems were encountered: machine maintenance and non-payment of fees for harrowing, but mechanization exacerbated bottlenecks in the flow of farm labour. The sexual division of labour in rice-cultivation systems rests on the complementarity of certain jobs, which was disturbed by mechanization. The introduction of tractors substituted male labour (ploughing and harrowing) and, given the larger areas cultivated, caused serious bottlenecks in the supply of female labour for weeding, harvesting, threshing and husking.

MacCormack (1978) observed some of the effects of mechanization in her work among the Sherbro along the southern coast of Sierra Leone, where the response among farmers was twofold; either cash was used to secure more wives, or there was increased cultivation of cash crops such as pineapples and bananas, which required little female labour. In 1976 bridewealth was some £50, compared with a rice milling machine which cost some £3,000; not only were additional wives a more viable option in the circumstances, but they were also able to reproduce the workforce and give greater continuity to Sherbro descent groups. In the swamp-rice areas four or five wives were not uncommon, and females were in excess by 149 per 100 males. In adjacent fishing villages, the reverse was the case and the excess of males was partly accounted for by the 'export' of women into rice-farming villages where they, or their husbands, had rights to farmland. Among the Sherbro there is cognatic descent and children have rights to land through mothers as well as fathers. Women, through marriage, are the means whereby migrant men can graft themselves onto a local descent group, and immigrants move into this area as clients hoping to become potential husbands; others come invoking a cognatic kinship tie with the 'owners' of the land.

Mechanized rice schemes have not produced the huge surpluses expected of them and Sierra Leone, once a net exporter of rice, is now importing up to 22,000 tons per annum. Yet swamp rice has become more important over the past fifty years and approximately 50 per cent of rice is grown on swamps of various kinds. The Sherbro case demonstrates both the problems of mechanized schemes and how adaptation to swamp rice has taken place within the domestic domain, which still forms the core of African agriculture.

The relative failure of the mechanized rice schemes has led to a greater interest in encouraging improved methods of swamp-rice cultivation through Integrated Rural Development projects, which are largely autonomous regional development authorities, linked to the Ministry of Agriculture. Two projects were started to give extension advice, improved farming inputs and infrastructures such as feeder roads, and eventually it is hoped to cover the whole of the country. Karimu and Richards (1980) have presented a preliminary survey of the Northern Area Project which gives some interesting insights into the response of farmers, especially how they manage and organize the supply of labour for swamp rice cultivation.

The assumptions which underpinned the integrated development project were that low output and productivity were due to poor technology and the persistence of upland-rice cultivation using rotational-fallowing, together with credit problems and the inadequacy of infrastructures, such as farm access roads. Also, the project planners believed that there was considerable underemployment of agricultural labour in northern Sierra Leone, a view which stems from an orthodoxy which was demolished in the late

1960s but apparently lingers on. Positivist development models of the 1950s emphasized the duality of underdeveloped economies, and the contrasts between the 'modern' and the 'traditional' sectors. In the latter the marginal productivity of agricultural labour was held to be either very low, or zero. Such conceptualizations were rooted in a misunderstanding of the demographic realities of Africa, and the production relations of peasant farmers; they were also derived from empirical research done in India and south-east Asia, where conditions are different. As we have observed earlier, there are important 'islands' of high population density and land shortage in Africa, especially around the larger towns; but, as Helleiner (1966) concluded, the most generally applicable model for Africa is one where labour is the constraint, not land.

Karimu and Richards (1980) demonstrate something of the chronic labour shortage which inhibits farming in Sierra Leone and which calls into question a policy of total commitment to labour-intensive swamp-rice cultivation. Also in Sierra Leone many rural areas have suffered high rates of out-migration to the diamond mining areas and the towns. Urban bias is also found in the way farmers transfer surpluses to the towns, as they try and educate their children; in the national context, there is price control of rice by the government who prefer imports to protect town-dwellers rather than letting rice prices rise to encourage farmers. Urban bias in the trajectory of economic growth has provided a focus for several authors of development studies, notably Lipton (1977).

In northern Sierra Leone, Karimu and Richards found that those household heads who were considered the best credit risk by the project were the ones who were wealthier in material and human resources, especially in terms of wives and children. But these same households were interested in long-term transfers of their resources out of farming into urban employment, trading and education of their children. These households were in the process of disengaging from the more traditional structures of village life, and looking for hired labour to work the more intensive rice swamps, rather than using festive or exchange labour. However, previous cycles of migration to the capital, Freetown, and diamond mining areas, together with the absence of landless peasants makes for a very limited labour supply, and causes serious problems for farmers engaged in improved swamp-rice farming. Perhaps one alternative strategy is to direct a greater proportion of inputs towards women.

The labour-supply problem for farmers can be vividly demonstrated by looking at the relative amounts of labour required for upland rice, and traditional and improved swamp cultivation. Upland rice requires some 180 man-days per hectare; about 200 man-days are needed for traditional (broadcast) swamp rice and 400 man-days for improved (transplanted) swamp rice. Although improved cultivation can yield up to 110 bushels per hectare, compared with 30–37 bushels per hectare for upland farms, the supply of labour is a serious constraint for project farmers, especially as the total labour inputs quoted above hide the peak periods of the busiest months. The response by project farmers, as reported by Karimu and Richards, is interesting and informative for future extensions of the scheme. Farmers with the median household of eight to nine members require some 90 bushels of rice per year and they can manage a maximum of 80 hours' labour per month. Improved swamp rice not only needs more labour, but, as only one or two varieties can be grown, there is no chance of staggering labour peaks (especially at harvest time), which is possible with the larger number of rice types grown on upland farms. The solution adopted by many farmers to the introduction of swamp rice, and the constraints of their labour supply, is to use their 80 hours' labour per month to grow two-thirds of their needs on upland farms, and one-third from local swamps. If farmers use this strategy, at no stage do they have to go beyond the average family's labour resources. Karimu and Richards have modelled the different labour inputs required for the three-rice farming systems and these are shown in Figure 6.1.

Efforts to increase food production in northern Ghana were started by the British during the Second World War to eliminate the need for imported food, especially in the south which was becoming a food deficit area. After Independence, the Nkrumah government began to invest in northern agriculture as the industrial, urban and rural economies of the south depended on marketed food surpluses produced outside the 'core' region of the Ghanaian economy (Shepherd, 1981). Their objective was to open up the shallow river valleys of the Northern Region for mechanized commercial rice farming by means of State-managed co-operatives organized by the United Ghana Farmers' Co-operative Council (UGFCC), which was the agricultural wing of the Congress People's Party. After Nkrumah, successive governments continued to invest State capital in northern rice farming, although the success of the schemes has been limited and has done little for peasant farmers. The nature and impact of agrarian changes in northern Ghana have been the subject of numerous commentaries, but there seems to be a consensus that State finance has been the means of buttressing and expanding capitalist relations of production (see, for example, Ansell, 1976; Miracle and Seidman, 1978; Shepherd, 1981; Van Hear, 1982).

In 1963 the main beneficiaries of the State co-operatives seem to have been small capitalists and trader–farmers in the principal northern town of Tamale, who began to enter mechanized farming through the tractor services provided by the UGFCC, which were designed to stimulate rice

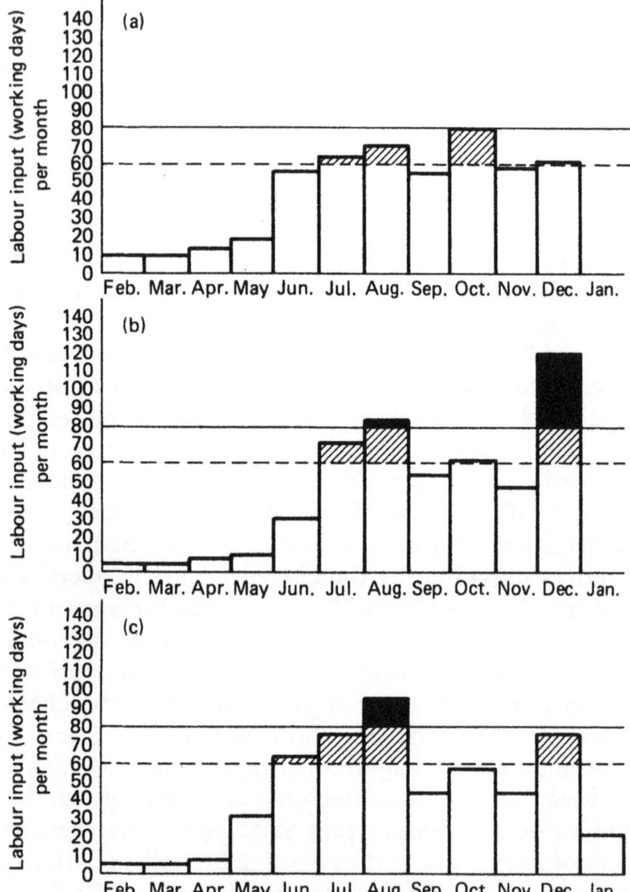

Fig. 6.1 The reduction of labour bottlenecks in rice-farming systems: three 'models' from Sierra Leone. (a) Two-thirds upland, one-third local swamp. (b) One-third upland, two-thirds local swamp. (c) Two-thirds improved swamp, one-third upland.

Source: Karimu and Richards (1980), p. 103.

production in the north. After the fall of Nkrumah in 1966, private entrepreneurship became the preferred government option and the Agricultural Development Bank selected relatively wealthy or influential farmers as good risks to develop rice and maize farming. It was these farmers who were able to take advantage of the dismantling of socialist agriculture, as they were able to buy up cheap machinery and take advantage of the pool of labour made redundant as State farms and co-operatives were disbanded. Capital has flowed into private rice cultivation from urban traders, merchants and civil servants, who in the 1960s were primarily northerners; but after 1973 increasing numbers of southerners entered farming (Shepherd, 1981). But as Van Hear (1982) has shown, these capitalist farmers failed to build up their labour forces from the skilled and semi-skilled workers they acquired from the State sector, as they paid rock-bottom wages and pursued cost-cutting practices, which eventually led to high turnover rates and conflict between labour and capital.

Farmers interested in cheap labour ignored the possibilities of developing the nucleus of an agricultural labour force provided by former State agencies and turned to the unemployed and partially employed in the towns who had little or no experience. Capitalist farmers required a core of permanent workers, especially tractor drivers, and a large army of casual workers for peak periods of weeding and harvesting. According to Van Hear (1982) permanent workers were paid in a variety of ways – cash, food, plots of land for private use, or a mixture of all three. Casual workers were recruited in 'by-day' labour centres, especially in Tamale, or along the roadsides. After the rice boom in 1978, farmers used increasing amounts of casual labour, often secondary-school boys and fourth-form leavers, together with women and week-end workers. As the proportion of casual workers increased, so the organization of farm labour altered.

Mixed groups of males, females and children paid daily wages gave way to more specialised workgroups on piece rates, as farmers tried to increase the quality and speed of work. Also, young men tended to form small groups who hired themselves out as contract workers; Van Hear (1982) has shown that as different groups resisted the attempts to extract larger surpluses from them so farmers explored new avenues of labour recruitment, including younger boys, non-local workers from further afield, casual workers, gang labour and even prison labour.

IRRIGATION SCHEMES IN NORTHERN NIGERIA

The penetration of agriculture by the State has played an important role in the emergence of capitalist relations of production in Ghana and increased the size of the agricultural labour force and 'semi-proletarianization'. Large-scale irrigation schemes in northern Nigeria financed by State capital have produced similar outcomes. The development of sophisticated water-control systems in the Chad, Kano and Sokoto-Rima river basins comprises the largest development schemes currently being undertaken in tropical Africa, and partly stems from the political necessity of redistributing some of the benefits of the oil boom towards the economically-less-advanced northern region. But they are aimed also at reducing imports of rice and wheat which feed the urban sector. In the context of the Third National Development Plan (1975–80) irrigated farming in the north is part of a general policy for rural areas, which seeks to raise rural incomes and narrow the differentials between rural and urban dwellers, to produce raw materials for industry and food for the urban sector, and to earn foreign exchange by exporting agricultural products. At a more local level the introduction of irrigated farming is seen as a means of curtailing the annual dry-season exodus of rural dwellers, as well as the more permanent drift into the towns. But, as Wallace (1979) observed, a basic assumption of this plan designed by the World Bank is that increased rural productivity will result in widespread improvement in rural incomes and welfare; the link between increased productivity and rural welfare remains ill-defined and unexplored. Another assumption of the plan is that the present low productivity is the result of illiterate peasants who lack modern technology and information on how to improve their farming.

The implementation of large irrigation schemes inevitably means that some people will be dispossessed of their land as the building of dams floods considerable acreages. The building of the Tiga dam in the Kano River basin led to the resettlement of some 13,000 people, while the Bakalori dam on the Sokoto River displaced some 18,000 inhabitants. Resettlement villages often have a poor water supply, and poor land: in heavily-populated areas such as the Kano and Sokoto regions land is scarce, and even if peasants have enough money to purchase land, good farms are frequently not available. The result may be that many resettled villagers leave and move on, or if they stay become agricultural labourers to offset the limited viability of the poor land they have been allocated. At the moment evidence of village desertion is limited, but after the building of the Kainji Dam there was a discernible depopulation of resettlement villages (Oyedipe, 1973).

For those on the schemes, the new technology of irrigated farming has proved difficult and for some farmers virtually impossible. Wallace (1979) has given some attention to the labour problems encountered by farmers on the Kano River project, and suggests that planners misunderstood the nature and organization of farm labour. It was assumed that the basic production unit was built around joint-families of the paternal and fraternal kind we discussed in Chapter 2 and again in Chapter 4. Under this kind of domestic organization, the head acquires unpaid labour from juniors, but as we observed such structures have undergone considerable erosion, not least in areas of high population density on the periphery of large towns such as Kano and Sokoto. Hausa farmers in the Kano Valley rely very much on non-family labour, such as young migrant workers, and local village labour.

The planners also failed to take into account the fact that the wet-and dry-season farm labour forces are not the same; dry-season labour migration is a long-established practice in Hausaland, and many farmers found that dry-season irrigated farming posed serious problems. Young men were not interested in farming during the dry season on irrigated land because the returns to labour were not sufficiently attractive, compared with jobs available in the expanding urban sector. This is partly a reflection of low prices and inadequate marketing arrangements offered by government and private traders. Planners paid little attention to how farmers might dispose of their produce, and, for example, almost up to the point of starting irrigated farming at Bakalori, the present author found that little consideration had been given to marketing. Other informants in Kano complained of having produced tomatoes from their irrigated land as part of the cropping schedule insisted upon by the River Valley Authority, only to have them rot by the roadside as they attempted to sell them; alternatively, they were bought up at rock-bottom prices by merchants with lorries coming out from Kano. The result of low prices is that men migrate, particularly from smaller, poorer households in the dry season, often with the approval of their families, who then resort to alternative and less-efficient sources of labour provided by young children and women to try and keep irrigated farms in production. If the land is not wholly farmed then it is rented out, either to more prosperous local farmers, or to urban traders and salaried government workers who then hire either local or migrant labour. Thus farmers with limited or seasonally-depleted labour resources rent out land and may themselves become part of the growing local labour market, as they find it difficult to continue farming in the dry season. Wallace (1978) found that in Waziri ward of Chiromawa town, 25 per cent of household heads, and 30 per cent of their dependent sons, had worked as wage labourers on the Kano River Valley project. Irrigated farming requires a range of inputs, such as fertilizers, water, seeds, and crop sprays, which are expensive for smaller farmers; and while two-year credits were offered by the Authority, no credits were available for hiring-in labour.

Renting of land was one outcome of irrigated farming in Kano, but to what extent land was being sold was not readily discernible. At Bakalori, on the Sokoto-Rima scheme, there were some indications of land sales even before plots were used (Wallace, 1980). On the Bakalori scheme farmers were allocated irrigated farms equivalent to their previous holdings of upland and floodland, minus 10 per cent for the absorption of land by the Authority for canals, roads and offices. Although this method of allocating new blocks of irrigated farmland is equitable, it also presents some farmers with a farm which is difficult to handle. For example, the cultivation of seven acres of wet-season upland and one acre of dry-season floodland is quite a different proposition from eight acres (minus 10 per cent) of irrigated land which has to be cultivated intensively throughout the year. The shortage of labour for irrigated farming may lead to land re-sales and renting, as farmers cannot cope, but it may be that some farmers are using less land on the new system to produce the same incomes and levels of subsistence as they had from the old system, and they have settled for this and rented surplus irrigated land, which together with off-farm work secures an adequate living. This of course does not fulfil the objective of the planners, who wish to raise rural productivity, farm incomes and State revenues. What does seem to have happened, in common with mechanized rice farming in Ghana, is the growth of capitalist farming, and an increase in the agricultural wage-labour force: the benefits, far from being widespread, have become limited to the richer rural farmers and urban entrepreneurs.

The effects of post-Independence development schemes have not been so dissimilar from the introduction of cash crops by the colonial régimes. What has happened in Ghana and Nigeria is the creation of opportunities for capitalist farming which are subsidized by the State. The element of risk-capital is almost nil, since farmers have access to land at low prices or rents, which has been improved to the tune of £3,000 per acre. Moreover there are the benefits of cheap inputs and credits. On the other hand it may be that the State is producing amounts of wheat, rice and vegetables which might reduce imports, or at least have a political pay-off in that certain classes or interest groups are well served by the schemes. Meanwhile many medium-scale and poorer farmers sit tight and adopt their own strategies for coping with new events, or households become increasingly 'proletarianized' as members enter the urban and agricultural labour markets. But if State capital has failed to transform the rural sector, what about more sweeping programmes of change built around socialist principles of production and distribution? One of the most radical and momentous programmes of rural change has been undertaken in Tanzania, using existing rural structures to build a new socialist order.

'UJAMAA' AND VILLAGIZATION IN TANZANIA

The Arusha Declaration of 1967 set forth the belief that Tanzanians should return to collective and communal values if their material conditions were to be rapidly and equitably improved. These values were to be found in the communal labour groups, *ujamaa*, which could be developed into a set of principles for living and working together, and provide a socialist framework for the transformation of Tanzania. The goals of the *ujamaa* policy were self-governing communities, a better use of rural labour, the ability to take advantage of economies of scale, to improve production, to disseminate new values, to avoid exploitation, to facilitate national planning, to raise the standard of living and to facilitate national defence. Apart from wishing to curtail individualistic tendencies encouraged by the colonial régime and the power of small-capitalist farmers, there was a concern not to make the same mistakes as large-scale development schemes, which were generally over-capitalized. Economies of scale were to be achieved through a larger labour force, using existing technology in the first instance, with the introduction of mechanization at a later stage (Hyden, 1980).

At first voluntaryism was accorded a high priority in the formation of the *ujamaa*, and there were some notable successes, but they were usually in lightly-populated and poorly-developed areas which had hitherto had a limited exposure to the market economy. As the majority of rural Tanzanians lived in dispersed settlements rather than villages, *ujamaa* needed a re-grouping of population to create effective communal labour forces working on communal farms. The creation of nucleated villages was an integral part of *ujamaa* policy, and villagization was seen as the means of introducing centralized services such as dispensaries, schools and extension services. Those in charge of planning believed that, to fulfil their functions, villages would have to be sited along roads, therefore the relocation of peasants would be not only into larger communities, but in specific places.

By 1970 it was apparent that *ujamaa* was proceeding slowly and a more positive attitude was required towards villagization if it was to become the key to the rapid development of *ujamaa*. In 1973 droughts underlined the natural constraints under which agriculturalists work and compulsory villagization was decided upon by the Tanzania African National Union (TANU), with the declared objective of re-locating the rural population by 1976. This comprised the largest resettlement in African history, and by 1974 2.5 million out of a total 13 million rural dwellers were settled in villages, although this did not mean that communal farming was widespread. The new villages were not popular, as they required longer journeys to fields, and labour time was being lost; also in some cases water supplies were not secure and farmers were moved into areas where soils were less than satisfactory. The farming ecology of close-nucleated settlements was different from former locations, and the concentration of cattle around villages and centralized water points can be destructive of the soil complex; while distance from farms meant a less effective watch on crop predators, such as baboons (Kjekhus, 1977). Roads became the focus of villages in order to provide viable services and infrastructures, but in some heavily-populated areas, such as the Highlands and the medium-density areas of Sukumaland, villagization was scarcely needed, as service centres at selected points would have reached the majority of dwellers (Cliffe, 1973).

Communal farming and villagization have met with considerable resistance, which has arisen from hasty planning, the conflict of interests between peasants and bureaucrats, and, not least, a misunderstanding of the fundamentals of peasant production. It is true that communal labour was widespread in Africa and still exists today, but it does not extend to the ownership or sharing of the product, except in special cases. As we saw in Chapter 5, the most important forms of communal labour are exchange workgroups operated on a reciprocal basis by a small number of farmers, who pool their labour, and who are quite clear about the 'rules of the game'. Although forms of communal work are part of rural tradition, the organization of labour and the distribution of the product is rooted in domestic groups built on principles of age, sex and kinship. It is true that in many instances rights to the use of land are vested in the village community, which determines its allocation; but once allocated the organization of farming and patterns of cropping are directed from *within* domestic groups. Rural communities often contain a good deal of tension between the interests of individual households and the interests of the community at large; there are forces which divide as well as bind the community. Exchange labour and festive workgroups may represent communal values, or the helping of one by another, but they are not primarily designed to produce surpluses; rather they exist to ensure an acceptable level of subsistence.

The semi-autonomy of domestic groups and their individualistic traits provided a ready basis for the emergence of small-commodity producers during the colonial period, and in some parts of Tanzania, such as the Highlands and Sukumaland, the market economy made substantial inroads. Planners seem to have taken little account of regional variations in the penetration of the non-capitalist economy by market relations, other than to see *ujamaa* as a way of counteracting this trend; the confrontation of capitalist and semi-capitalist farmers became more of an issue as *ujamaa* programmes proceeded. Yet there was sufficient awareness of peasant attitudes to allow *ujamaa* villagers the right to cultivate their own private plots; but as elsewhere private plots have become something of a stumbling-block to full-time peasant commitment to community and national interests.

The hours worked on communal farms show tremendous fluctuations, although there are few small-scale in-depth studies of the workings of *ujamaa*, especially on a comparative basis. Sumra (1979) provides some insights into the workings of communal farms in a survey of several villages in Handemi District. More workers turned out for communal farming when food was short, and numbers varied according to the type of job, whereas under traditional systems of labour exchange jobs were done as required by the host. The timing of work on communal farms was less than satisfactory, as clearing tended to take place after it was completed on private plots, and once the rains were under way weeding and vermin control were poorly done for the same reason. Communal farms devoted to commercial crops such as cotton also suffered, because insufficient workers were available for intensive and continuous jobs such as spraying and picking. Labour bottlenecks have become a constraint on production levels, just as they have in other farming systems, but the conflict has arisen not between food staples and commercial crops, but between private and communal plots. Sumra (1979) suggested that perhaps communal farms should have been devoted to certain tree crops, or animals and poultry, where labour demands were complementary; alternatively, labour on communal farms should be compulsory, or confined to committed members of the village.

In the West Lake Region, Boesen (1979) encountered similar examples of irregular and fluctuating labour supplies on communal farms. Less than half the potential working days in the season were spent on communal farms, and then the working day was reduced to around four or five hours. During any one day only one-third, or one-half, of the potential labour force actually came to work on the farm. Boesen found that many villagers felt that communal farms were rather a waste of time, and that yields were poor, a feeling which grew out of their own lack of firm commitment on the one hand, and poor management on the other. The organization of labour on communal farms is not easy and requires considerable managerial effort and expertise. The recording of the quantity and the quality of work and the correct reward is difficult, and in many instances attendance becomes the only criterion.

The food requirements of households often lack a direct equivalence to the input they can muster; a small number of active adults with a large number of young or old dependants is in a stage of imbalance, although formerly they could resort to adjusting working hours, calling on their kin or using labour-exchange groups. It must be stressed again that labour exchange was a means of pooling labour inputs and, apart from food and drink, did not affect the product. Also labour exchange works best where small numbers are involved, say half a dozen, whereas the planners of *ujamaa* villages set much higher ceilings and it was this that exacerbated the organizational problems (Barker, 1979). Smaller communal groups of about thirty seemed to work much better, because there was cohesiveness and mutual trust, which made record-keeping irrelevant. When planners demanded a lower limit of 250 families per village, or about 1,000 inhabitants, their objectives were being determined not by the requirements of efficient farm labour, but of the thresholds for the provision of certain services.

Communal farms and farming in many villages have become little more than symbolic gestures, and the necessary strategy for the acquisition of services and farming inputs provided by the State. Communal farming raised many doubts in the minds of peasants as to its objectives and benefits; if they work harder who will benefit – the Government, bureaucrats, urban dwellers or foreigners? The latter qualification became more apparent as there was a shift towards export crops in the mid 1970s, in order to increase state revenues. Also, village members were never clear about their rights to accumulated wealth and collective property; under traditional relations of production there were general, if not unquestioned, rights to land and property, and if divorced wives or brothers left a household, rights and responsibilities were understood.

It is not surprising that peasants stuck so closely to their private plots, because they were able to retain control over their labour and its product, in the manner to which they were accustomed as small-commodity producers. Also they were familiar with particular pieces of ground which their families had farmed for generations. This was particularly true of smaller and poorer domestic groups, who had most to lose from investing their limited labour time in a communal enterprise from which the returns were far from certain, or appropriate. Better-off households had spare labour and could afford the risk, and so this was another reason for the fluctuating levels of labour found within communal enterprises (Hyden, 1980). Such attitudes are entrenched in concepts of anteriority and posteriority and the production and reproduction of domestic groups, controlled by individuals, not elected village bodies. It is in this context that peasant resistance to villagization must be seen.

SUMMARY

The penetration of agriculture by the State has taken a variety of forms and has been based on different ideological premises. Both State capitalism and State socialism have faced similar problems, inasmuch as they have had to deal with a multitude of domestic groups shaped by age, sex and kin, which have become adapted to small-commodity production, and who are less than willing to meet national plans and objectives. Hyden (1980) has referred to an 'uncaptured peasantry' who have too many 'exit options', compared with the majority of those living in modern capitalist and socialist States who have little choice in offering their labour to entrepreneurs, or State managers. The State can easily initiate new agrarian policies, as there is limited opposition from a merchant- or land-owning class, but the power to make policies stick is hollow where the State exercises minimal control over the peasant economy. There are those (for example, Dumont, 1969) who believe that the quantum jump from pre-capitalist to either capitalist or socialist large-scale farming, is too great without an intervening historical process of change which involves small-capitalist production. On the other hand it has been suggested that, in socialist experiments, it is the ideology which has been imperfect, and that the crucial problem is one of bureaucratic control, and the take-over of agriculture by a new class of bureaucrats operating under an umbrella of pseudo-socialism. Meanwhile, whether to implement change on a broad front, or to select particular classes or cadres in specific geographical regions as agents of change, remains a contentious issue.

CONCLUSION

Most Africans win part of their living from the land and, despite the rapid pace of urbanization, the continent is primarily a myriad of small rural households. Agriculture remains small-scale and above all labour-intensive. This is not to deny that technical innovations have had some impact, but the most significant changes have been in the organization of labour to produce new crops and marketable surpluses. While some farmers may have improved their farming through the use of fertilizers and ox-ploughs, for the most part it has been those with access to labour, either domestic or hired, who have managed to produce and reproduce their material conditions adequately, as well as to produce surpluses for local and international markets.

Traditionally, farming was about the cultivation of crops, using production relationships held together by joint-production and consumption. Not all traditional groups were extended ones, yet co-operation based on paternal, maternal and filial relationships was commonplace. Although such groups had well-developed systems of dependence and obligation, they also contained the seeds of individualism, inasmuch as time was available for personal farms and employment in crafts and trading. Adequate supplies of food could be produced without every day or hour being used while, in some parts of the continent, the development of pre-colonial states and trading networks meant there was a well-established market economy and the social division of labour. But it was the penetration of European merchant capital and colonialism which accelerated, or in some cases activated, latent individualism through the cultivation of new commercial crops, which brought about new relations of production.

The development of new crops required either an intensification of effort from within domestic groups or the means of acquiring external sources of labour. This was particularly important when export crops were grown simultaneously with food staples. Intensification from within meant longer working hours, or in some cases was achieved by altering the internal division of labour. As men have become more involved in commercial cropping and non-farm occupations, so women have become increasingly responsible for the cultivation of food staples. This is especially true in those areas where out-migration of men is persistent, and it could be argued that the expansion of commercial cropping and the industrial labour force has been built on the backs of women farmers.

The intensification and reallocation of labour within domestic groups is not the only method of increasing the labour supply; local or long-distance migrant labour can be hired, which means there are net transfers of labour from one area, and from one group, to another. Such transfers are the product of regional specialization, as well as new social relationships in rural communities and increased economic differentiation as capitalist relations of production have gained ground. The use of hired labour, the quantity used, and under what contractual terms, are often ways of differentiating farmers, and many hired workers if not 'landless' are 'land-poor'. Many villages now contain small semi-capitalist farmers who hire wage labour and invest in capital improvements and purchase land. The appearance of wealthier farmers may be the result of their access to resources through their traditional roles in village communities, or through personal energy and initiative. In non-capitalist societies there is a differentiation among domestic groups, for example, those who belong to founding lineages, or who are functionaries (such as priests), all of whom have greater access to land or labour through work days given to them by villagers, or who formerly had large numbers of slaves. Asymmetric relationships were not absent in pre-colonial Africa and non-capitalist societies contain elements of conflict as well as homogeneity. But subsequently the initial advantages of certain groups were transformed to meet new circumstances as the market economy became more pervasive and individuals worked for wages, rather than providing obligatory labour to their kinsmen or making contributions to communal systems based on labour exchange.

On the other hand, richer farmers have also emerged who are not related to previous structures of prestige and influence; often they are men who have been successful as traders, or even ex-slaves who were more flexible and entered into new commercial farming enterprises more readily than others. It is also true that now some farmers have greater access to resources and immunity from disaster through political clientage linked to administrative hierarchies and political parties. Economic differentiation in rural communities arises from a kaleidoscopic range of forces operating at the local level, set within a framework of larger structural shifts in the political economy which have created conditions for the erosion of traditional systems of organization and control.

The increased commoditization of agricultural production and the growth of non-farm employment have been part of the decline of larger domestic groups and joint agricultural production. Domestic groups have become looser and smaller, and in many parts of Africa labour co-operation among kinsmen has become skeletal. Fission occurs at an earlier stage, for example, immediately upon marriage; paternal-based groups are now less common and fraternal ones have a shorter lifetime. Smaller domestic groupings are often much more susceptible to the effects of adverse dependency ratios, illness, accident and premature death, as well as to adverse market conditions, droughts and the traumas of planned agrarian change. It is often smaller, poorer households that are drawn into farm labouring, while larger, more prosperous ones have members in nearby towns, engaged in semi-skilled jobs, the professions, or trading. When farm prices are held down by government agencies or traders, it often means that the product market is much less rewarding than the labour market; perhaps most frequently it means that a mixed strategy is required for household production and reproduction, which is why some members, usually men, become wage labourers, and increasing amounts of farm work devolve upon women, children and older people.

Seasonal migration and daily commuting to nearby towns are in many instances the means whereby peasants have come to terms with changes in the local and national political economy from colonial times onwards. But high levels of personal mobility, whether they arise from personal acquisitiveness or economic necessity, are not really compatible with domestic joint-production where labour-intensive agriculture is optimized under co-operative conditions of working (Isaacs, 1982). Consequently mobility is instrumental in the decline of extended domestic groups, and smaller households have circuits of production and reproduction which rely on external earnings of migrant workers as well as on their internal production of crops for subsistence or for the commodity market. One can make a distinction between domestic production groups, where the redistribution of labour occurs to offset premature death, illness or specific phases of their development cycles, and domestic groups which have been heavily penetrated by the market economy, where the scale of mobility has changed because it now rests on new social relations of production.

The shift towards agricultural wage labour has created what have been described as 'semi-' or 'proto-proletarians', and migrant labour reserves have become prominent features of the social and economic landscape of tropical Africa. An agricultural wage-paid labour force employed by small semi-capitalist farmers is probably more widespread than is often appreciated, and around the fringes of large towns the use of hired farm workers seems to be increasing. But it would be wrong not to urge some caution with scenarios of 'proletarianization'; many urban and rural wage earners still retain their rights to land, and the shift into wage labour need not be either complete or a one-way process.

Rural Africa is now characterized by heterogeneous communities where farm labour can be mobilized, controlled and rewarded in a variety of ways, and consequently the mobility of farm labour is of a high order. Both neo-classical analyses, such as the 'vent for surplus' theory, and Marxist formulations of models of production and peasantization, pay little attention to the redistribution of labour, which is an integral part of maintaining agricultural production where labour-intensive farming is the norm. Agricultural production in Africa is built around borrowing, lending, sharing and hiring, which on the one hand maintain equity and homogeneity, and on the other promote inequality and conflict within rural communities.

In some areas designated for rural development, the conflict between labour and State, or the bureaucracy representing the State, has become an important dimension of agrarian labour relations. The attempt to transform semi-subsistence farmers and peasant commodity producers either into State employees or capitalist wage labour has encountered considerable resistance and subversion of the aims of the planners. State capitalism has often increased economic differentiation and accelerated capitalist relations of production and levels of landlessness. Programmes of socialist reconstruction and development have met with resistance to communal farming, and private plots have often been cultivated at the expense of collective enterprise.

Access to land and the control of the means of production by peasants have not been entirely destroyed by either state bureaucracies or capitalist penetration; 'small' remains subversive of government policy, and equally peasants have not been irreversibly controlled by other social classes. Peasants remain 'uncaptured' either by capitalist or socialist programmes of rural change and development. The modern work ethic of capitalist and socialist societies has not been fully internalized by peasants; work is not universally an end in itself, or a habit controlled by managers and the work environment (Hyden, 1980). Misconceptions about agricultural production and the social relations of production have led to some bizarre episodes in the realm of rural development planning. Questions about production and production relationships are not just academic issues, as they have a vital relevance for programmes of rural change.

From some standpoints, agricultural production and the organization of farm labour look relatively simple; from others they appear to be complex and fluid. Many rural communities embrace a spectrum of productive relationships which extend from corporate production by kinship groups, of joint-families, to capitalist farmers and agricultural wage labourers. Despite the general structural changes in the political economy during the nineteenth and twentieth centuries, considerable diversity can be found at regional and local levels, while changes in the labour process have proceeded erratically, often in a non-linear fashion, and the transformation of agrarian communities by capitalist and socialist forces has only been partial. Change has been patchy both over time and space, and the forms of agricultural labour encountered can alter quite quickly from one region to another. Consequently it is not easy to fit general theory to specific African situations, nor to encapsulate the spatial shifts and variations which occur regionally and locally.

The generality of propositions and concepts and their dependence on historical and spatial contingency has led some writers to argue for the dismantling of 'grand theories' into lower-level concepts which have greater generality and specificity. For example, Kitching (1980) disclaims the usefulness of mode-of-production analysis, articulation of modes and class theory in African situations, and favours lower-order concepts such as mode of appropriation of surplus labour, mode of appropriation of nature, and division of labour and circulation (commodities and money), which are more applicable to any historical situation where commodity production occurs. As we have suggested, in tropical Africa today production relationships are varied and flexible and categories such as 'pre-capitalist', 'peasant' and 'proletarianization' need handling with care. Although there are unmistakable signs of the development of capitalist relations in agriculture, and economic differentiation among producers, on balance small-commodity production is probably the most widespread category in rural communities; that is, when agricultural production is in the hands of individuals or domestic groups, who still exercise some control over their means of production and sell the product of their labour in markets, using the money to buy other products. Many households hire occasional labour, and labour surpluses are transferred from one household to another, although this does not involve the control of the means of production by the hirers of those hired. Equally those who appropriate the labour of others in villages may do so because their labour (or part of it) is being appropriated by others for whom they work, in agriculture or industry; the exploiters are also exploited.

But agricultural production and production relationships do not take place in an ecological vacuum and, in situations where production techniques are relatively direct, it is important to have some understanding of how farming relates to the physical environment. This is not to imply a legitimization of inequalities in society, or of the differences between the status of men and women on environmental and biological grounds, but of identifying the respective effects of nature and society in agricultural production, and how each affects the other. While it is dangerous to attribute to 'nature' what is in reality due to 'society', it should not blind us to the dangers of manic triumphalism, whereby nature presents no obstacles if only productive forces can be organized properly, irrespective of the social cost. Farm labour is involved in the physical transformation of nature to secure material wants and needs, but it is also simultaneously informed by ideas which may be used to monitor the results. Agricultural practice requires communication among those concerned, which may take symbolic forms or otherwise, and work involves a sharing of meaning among people (Sayer, 1983). Development planners and academic commentators have often ignored both peasant 'modes of environmental perception' and how the participants understand farming and farm work.

If we are to edge towards an understanding of agricultural production, then we must confront the production process and the social relations into which people enter to secure their present and future needs, and how they perceive their efforts. Research is required which helps peasants to problematize issues and codify and articulate them at household and community levels. Peasants might be helped to internalize the answers to questions raised by themselves as well as by researchers and government agencies (see Freire, 1970; Hyden, 1980). Also, it is necessary to look at production and production relations as they exist now, in specific parts of the continent, and at how they have evolved, but without romanticizing African traditions. The difficulty in understanding rural society is the one encountered throughout the social sciences: that of reconciling individual actions and perceptions with the larger structural forces of society and State, and the manner in which these contradictions have developed historically. There is an opposition between 'subjectivism' and 'objectivism' and between the observed regularities of social action (the structure) and experiential reality of reasoning, purposeful human actors. But any solution to this conflict must at the same time provide a properly historical explanation by specifying the social conditions under which the structure will be reproduced or, conversely, will be rapidly transformed (Bourdieu, 1977; Garnham and Williams, 1980). It is within this kind of framework that one can profitably engage in the study of rural society in Africa and of that most important part of it, the agricultural labour force.

BIBLIOGRAPHY

Akenda-Ondoga, V. J. 1980. An Economic Study of Production Organization and Labour Use Among Smallholders in Nile Province, Uganda. Ph.D. thesis. Cornell University.

Amerena, P. M. J. 1982. Farmers' Participation in the Cash Economy: Case Studies of Two Settlements in the Kano Close-Settled Zone of Nigeria. Ph.D. thesis. University of London.

Ansell, D. J. 1976. *Mechanized Rice Production in Northern Ghana.* London: Barclays Bank.

Apthorpe, R. 1977. A Comment on Andrew Pearse's Review of Global-2, *Development and Change*, 8: 370–3.

Balandier, G. 1963. *Sociologie Actuelle de l'Afrique Noire.* Paris: P. U. F.

Barker, J. 1979. The Debate on Rural Socialism in Tanzania. In B. U. Mwansasu and C. Pratt (eds.), *Towards Socialism in Tanzania.* Dar es Salaam: Tanzania Publishing House.

Barret, V., Lassiter, G., Wilcock, D., Baker, D. and Crawford, E. 1982. *Animal Traction in Eastern Upper Volta: A Technical and Institutional Analysis.* East Lansing: Michigan State University, Department of Agricultural Economics, MSU International Development Paper No. 4.

Baumann, H. 1928. The Division of Work According to Sex in African Hoe-Culture. *Africa*, 1(3): 289–319.

Berry, S. S. 1975. *Cocoa, Custom and Socio-Economic Change in Rural Western Nigeria.* Oxford: Clarendon Press.

Bijimi, I. A. 1963. *Traditional Land Tenure Surveys: Report on Part of Zaria Province.* Zaria, Nigeria: Institute of Administration, Ahmadu Bello University.

Binns, J. A. 1981. The Dynamics of Third World Food Production

Systems: An Evaluation of Change and Development in the Rural Economy of Sierra Leone. Ph.D. thesis. University of Birmingham.

Birmingham, D. and Martin, P. M. (eds.). 1983. *History of Central Africa*, vols 1 and 2. Harlow: Longmans, Green.

Boesen, J. 1979. Tanzania: from Ujamaa to Villagization. In B. U. Mwansasu and C. Pratt (eds.), *Towards Socialism in Tanzania*. Dar es Salaam: Tanzania Publishing House.

Boserup, E. 1965. *The Conditions of Agricultural Growth: The Economics of Agrarian Change Under Population Pressure*. London: Allen and Unwin.

1970. *Woman's Role in Economic Development*. New York: St Martins Press.

Bourdieu, P. 1977. *Outline of a Theory of Practice*. Cambridge: Cambridge University Press.

Brown, D. 1984. Production in Pre-Colonial Klowe (Liberia), *Africa*, 54 (2): 29–47.

Buntjer, B. 1973. Rural Society in the Zaria Area: The Changing Structure of Gandu. *Samaru Research Bulletin*, 80. Samaru, Nigeria: Institute of Agricultural Research.

Chambers, R., Longhurst, R., Bradley, D. and Feachem, R. 1979. Seasonal Dimensions to Rural Poverty: Analysis and Practical Implications. Discussion Paper 142. Sussex, England: Institute of Development Studies.

Charsley, S. R. 1976. *The Silika*: A Cooperative Labour Institution, *Africa*, 46(1): 34–47.

Clarke, J. 1980. Peasantization and Landholding: A Nigerian Case Study. In M. Klein (ed.), *Peasants in Africa: Historical and Contemporary Perspectives*. London and Beverly Hills: Sage Publications.

1981. Small-Scale Cash Crop Production in South-Western Nigeria, *Africa*, 51(4): 807–23.

Clayton, E. S. 1968. Opportunity Costs and Decision Making in Peasant Agriculture, *Netherlands Journal of Agricultural Science*, 16(4): 232–43.

Cleave, J. H. 1974. *African Farmers: Labour Use in the Development of Smallholder Agriculture*. New York: Praeger.

Cliffe, L. 1973. The Policy of Ujamaa Vijijini and the Class Struggle in Tanzania. In L. Cliffe and J. S. Saul (eds.), *Socialism in Tanzania*,

Dar es Salaam: East African Publishing House.

1977. Rural Class Formation in East Africa, *Journal of Peasant Studies*, 4(2): 195–224.

Cohen, R. 1976. From Peasants to Workers. In P. C. W. Gutkind and I. Wallerstein (eds.), *The Political Economy of Contemporary Africa*. London and Beverly Hills: Sage Publications.

Cohen, R. and Hutton, C. 1975. African Peasants and Resistance to Change: A Reconsideration of Sociological Approaches. In I. Oxaal, T. Barnett and D. Booth (eds.), *Beyond the Sociology of Development*. London: Routledge and Kegan Paul.

Collinson, M. P. 1972. *Farm Management in Peasant Agriculture: A Handbook for Rural Development Planning in Africa*. New York: Praeger.

1982. *Farming Systems Research in Eastern Africa: the Experience of CIMMYT and Some National Agricultural Research Services 1976–81*. East Lansing: Michigan State University, Department of Agricultural Economics, MSU International Development Paper No. 3.

Colvin, L. G., Ba, C., Barry, B., Faye, J., Hamer, A., Soumah, M. and Sow, F. 1981. *The Uprooted of the Western Sahel: Migrants' Quest for Cash in the Senegambia*. New York: Praeger.

Cooper, F. 1982a. Islam and Cultural Hegemony: The Ideology of Slaveowners on The East African Coast. In Lovejoy (ed.), *The Ideology of Slavery*. London and Beverly Hills: Sage Publications.

Coulibaby, S., Gregory, J. and Piche, V. 1980. *Les Migrations Voltaiques*, Tome I. Haute-Volta: Institut National de la Statistique et de la Demographie.

Cruise O'Brien, D. 1979. Ruling Class and Peasantry in Senegal, 1960–76: The Politics of a Monocrop Economy. In R. Cruise O'Brien (ed.), *The Political Economy of Underdevelopment: Dependency in Senegal*. London and Beverly Hills: Sage Publications.

Crummey, D. and Stewart, C. C. (eds.), 1981. *Modes of Production in Africa: The Precolonial Era*. London and Beverly Hills: Sage Publications.

Davies, H. J. R. 1976. *Town and Country in North Central State of Nigeria*. Samaru, Nigeria: Institute of Agricultural Research.

De Schlippe, P. 1956. *Shifting Cultivation in Africa: The Zande System of Agriculture*. London: Routledge and Kegan Paul.

Dey, J. M. 1980. Women and Rice in the Gambia: The Impact of Irrigated Rice Development Projects on the Farming System. Ph.D. thesis. University of Reading.

Dumont, R. 1969. *Tanzanian Agriculture after the Arusha Declaration.* Dar es Salaam: Ministry of Economic Affairs and Development Planning.

Eicher, C. K. and Baker, D. C. 1982. *Research on Agricultural Development in Sub-Saharan Africa: A Critical Survey.* East Lansing: Michigan State University, Department of Agricultural Economics, MSU International Development Paper No. 1.

Ennew, J., Hirst, P. and Tribe, K. 1977. 'Peasantry' as an Economic Category, *Journal of Peasant Studies*, 4(4): 295–322.

Erasmus, C. J. 1956. Culture Structure and Process: The Occurrence and Disappearance of Reciprocal Farm Labour, *Southwestern Journal of Anthropology*, 12(4): 444–69.

Evans, A. C. 1960. Studies of Inter-Cropping, *East African Agricultural and Forestry Journal*, 26(1): 1–10.

Fortes, M. 1958. Introduction in J. Goody (ed.), *The Development Cycle in Domestic Groups.* Cambridge: Cambridge University Press.

Freire, P. 1970. *The Pedagogy of The Oppressed.* New York: Herder and Herder.

Galletti, R., Baldwin, K. D. S. and Dina, I. O. 1956. *Nigerian Cocoa Farmers: An Economic Survey of Yoruba Cocoa-Farming Families.* London: Oxford University Press.

Garnham, N. and Williams, R. 1980. Pierre Bourdieu and Sociology of Culture, *Media and Culture*, 209–23.

Goddard, A. D. 1973. Changing Family Structures Among the Rural Hausa. *Samaru Research Bulletin* 196. Samaru, Nigeria: Institute of Agricultural Research.

Goddard, A. D., Fine, J. C. and Norman, D. W. 1971. *A Socio-Economic Survey of Three Villages in the Sokoto Close-Settled Zone. Vol. 1: Land and People.* Samaru, Nigeria: Institute of Agricultural Research.

Goddard, S. 1965. Town-Farm Relationships in Yorubaland: A Case Study from Oyo, *Africa*, 35: 21–9.

Godelier, M. 1977. *Perspectives in Marxist Anthropology.* Cambridge: Cambridge University Press.

Goody, J. R. (ed.) 1958. *The Development Cycle in Domestic Groups.* Cambridge: Cambridge University Press.

Guyer, J. I. 1980. Female Farming and the Evolution of Food Production Patterns Among the Beti of South-Central Cameroon, *Africa*, 50(4): 341–56.

1984. Naturalism in Models of African Production. *Man*, 19(3): 371–88.

Harris, J. (ed.). 1982. *Rural Development: Theories of Peasant Economy and Agrarian Change*. London: Hutchinson.

Hart. K. 1982. *The Political Economy of West African Agriculture*. Cambridge: Cambridge University Press.

Haswell, M. R. 1953. *Economics of Agriculture in a Savannah Village*. London: HMSO.

1963. *The Changing Pattern of Economic Activity in a Gambian Village*. London: HMSO.

Helleiner, G. K. 1966. Typology in Development Theory: The Land Surplus Economy, *Food Research Institute Studies*, 6(2): 181–94.

Heymer, S. 1970. Capital and Capitalists. Foreward to P. Hill (1970), *Studies in Rural Capitalism in West Africa*. Cambridge: Cambridge University Press.

Hill, P. 1963. *The Migrant Cocoa Farmers of Southern Ghana: A Study in Rural Capitalism*. Cambridge: Cambridge University Press.

1970. *Studies in Rural Capitalism in West Africa*. Cambridge: Cambridge University Press.

1972. *Rural Hausa: A Village and a Setting*. Cambridge: Cambridge University Press.

1976. From Slavery to Freedom: The Case of Farm Slavery in Nigerian Hausaland, *Comparative Studies in Society and History*, 18: 395–426.

1977. *Population, Prosperity and Poverty: Rural Kano, 1900 and 1970*. Cambridge: Cambridge University Press.

Hilton, R. H. 1975. *The English Peasantry in the Later Middle Ages*. Oxford: Clarendon Press.

Hogendorn, J. 1978. *Nigerian Groundnut Exports: Origins and Early Development*. Zaria, Nigeria: Ahmadu Bello University Press.

Hopkins, A. G. 1976. Clio-Antics: A Horoscope for African Economic History. In C. Fyfe (ed.), *African Affairs Since 1945: A Tribute to Basil Davidson*. London: Longmans, Green.

Hyden, G. 1980. *Beyond Ujamaa in Tanzania: Underdevelopment and an Uncaptured Peasantry*. London: Heinemann.

Isaacs, B. L. 1982. Economic Development and Subsistence Farming: The

Case of the Mende of Upper Bambara Chiefdom, Sierra Leone, *Central Issues in Anthropology*, 4(1): 1–20.

Jeng, A. 1978. An Economic History of the Gambian Groundnut Industry, 1830–1924: The Evolution of an Export Economy. Ph.D. thesis. University of Birmingham.

Jewsiewicki, B. and Bawele, M. M. 1982. The Social Context of Slavery in Equatorial Africa During the 19th and 20th Centuries. In P. Lovejoy (ed.), *The Ideology of Slavery*, pp. 72–98. London and Beverly Hills: Sage Publications.

Jones, W. O. 1959. *Manioc in Africa*. Ithaca: Cornell University Press.

Kaberry, P. M. 1952. *Women of the Grassfields. A Study of the Economic Position of Women in Bamenda, British Cameroon*. London: HMSO.

Kahn, J. S. and Llobera, J. R. (eds.). 1981. *The Anthropology of Pre-Capitalist Societies*. London: Macmillan.

Karimu, J. and Richards, P. 1980. The Northern Area Integrated Agricultural Development Programme. Occasional Paper No. 3. (new series) SOAS: Department of Geography.

Kayser, B., Fahem, A. K. and Pain, M. 1981. Cherte du Manioc et Pauvreté Paysanne dans le Bas-Zaire, *Cahiers d'Outre-Mer*, 134: 97–110.

Kitching, G. 1980. *Class and Economic Change in Kenya: The Making of an African Petite Bourgeoisie 1905–1970*. London and New Haven: Yale University Press.

Kjekhus, H. 1977. The Tanzanian Villagization Policy: Implementational Lessons and Ecological Dimensions, *Canadian Journal of African Studies*, 11(2): 282.

Klein, M. A. (ed.). 1980. *Peasants in Africa: Historical and Contemporary Perspectives*. London and Beverly Hills: Sage Publications.

Kongstad, P. and Mönsted, M. 1980. *Family Labour and Trade in Western Kenya*. Uppsala: Scandanavian Institute of African Studies.

La Fontaine, J. S. (ed.). 1978. *Sex and Age as Principles of Social Differentiation*. London: Academic Press.

Law, R. 1978. In Search of a Marxist Perspective in Pre-colonial Tropical Africa, *Journal of African History*, 19(3): 441–52.

Levi, J. and Havinden, M. 1982. *Economics of African Agriculture*. Harlow: Longmans, Green.

Lipton, M. 1977. *Why Poor People Stay Poor: A Study of Urban Bias in World Development*. London: Temple Smith.

Little, K. 1967. *The Mende of Sierra Leone*. London: Routledge and Kegan Paul.

Lovejoy, P. (ed.). 1981. *The Ideology of Slavery*. London and Beverly Hills: Sage Publications.

Luning, H. A. 1967. *Economic Aspects of Low Labour-Income Farming*. Agricultural Research Reports 699. Wageningen: Centre for Agricultural Publications and Documentation.

MacCormack, C. P. 1978. The Cultural Ecology of Production: Sherbro Coast and Hinterland, Sierra Leone. In D. Green, C. Haselgrove and M. Springs (eds.), *Social Organization and Settlement: Contributions from Anthropology, Archaeology and Geography*. BAR International Series (Supplementary) 47.

Main, H. A. C. 1981. Time-Space-Study of Daily Activity in Urban Sokoto, Nigeria. Ph.D. thesis. University of Liverpool.

Mayer, P. 1951. Agricultural Cooperation by Neighbourhood Groups Among the Gusii. In P. Mayer, *Two Studies in Applied Anthropology in Kenya*. Colonial Research Studies No. 3. London: HMSO.

Meillasoux, C. 1964. *Anthropologie Économique des Gouro de Cote d'Ivoire: de L'économie de Subsistence à l'agriculture Commerciale*. Paris: Mouton.

1972. From Reproduction to Production. *Economy and Society*, 1(1): 93–105.

1981. *Maidens, Meal and Money: Capitalism and the Domestic Community*. Cambridge: Cambridge University Press.

Mintz, S. W. 1979. The Rural Proletariat and the Problem of Rural Proletarian Consciousness. In R. Cohen, P. C. W. Gutkind and P. Brazier (eds.), *Peasants and Proletarians*. London: Hutchinson.

Miracle, M. and Seidman, A. 1978. *Agricultural Cooperatives and Quasi-Cooperatives in Ghana 1961–65*. Madison: University of Wisconsin Land Tenure Centre.

Mönsted, M. 1977, *The Changing Division of Labour Within Families in Kenya*. Copenhagen: Centre for Development Research.

Moore, M. P. 1975. Cooperative Labour in Peasant Agriculture, *Journal of Peasant Studies*, 2: 270–91.

Mortimore, M. J. 1975. Peri-Urban Pressures. In R. P. Moss and R. J. A. Rathbone (eds.), *The Population Factor in African Studies*. London: University of London Press.

Mortimore, M. J. and Wilson, J. 1965. *Land and People in the Kano Close-Settled Zone*. Dept. of Geography Occasional Paper No. 1, Ahmadu Bello University, Zaria, Nigeria.

Mwima-Mudeenya, E. 1978. A Neglected Component of Developing Economics; Small Scale Production and Employment in Uganda. Ph.D. thesis. Cornell University.

Njoku, A. O. and Karr, G. L. 1973. Labour and Upland Rice Production, *Journal of Agricultural Economics*, 24(2): 289–99.

Norman, D. W. 1972. *An Economic Study of Three Villages in Zaria Province*. Vols. 1 and 2. Samaru, Nigeria: Institute of Agricultural Research.

1974. Rationalizing Mixed Cropping Under Indigenous Conditions: The Example of Northern Nigeria, *Journal of Development Studies*, 11: 3–21.

1980. The Farming Systems Approach: Relevancy for the Small Farmer. East Lansing: Michigan State University, Department of Agricultural Economics, MSU Rural Development Paper No. 5.

O'Keefe, P., Wisner, B. and Baird, A. 1977. Kenyan Underdevelopment: A Case Study of Proletarianization. In P. O'Keefe and B. Wisner (eds.), *Landuse and Development*. London: International African Institute.

O'Leary, M. 1983. Population, Economy and Domestic Groups: The Kitui Case, *Africa*, 53(1): 64–76.

Olusanya, P. 1972. Socio-economic Disparities and Internal Migration in Nigeria: Mass Exodus of Village Dwellers to Yoruba Towns. Eleventh International African Seminar on Modern Migrations in Western Africa. Dakar: Institut du Développement Economique et Plonification.

Oyedipe, F. P. A. 1973. Problems of Socio-Economic Adjustment of Resettlers in Nigeria. In A. L. Mabogunje (ed.), *Kainji: Man-Made Lake: Socio-Economic Conditions*. Ibadan: Nigerian Institute of Social and Economic Research.

Palmer, R. and Parsons, N. (eds.), 1977. *The Roots of Rural Poverty in Central and Southern Africa*. London: Heinemann.

Pearce, R. 1983. Sharecropping: Towards a Marxist View, *Journal of Peasant Studies*, 10: 42–69.

Pélissier, P. 1966. *Les Paysans du Senegal: les Civilisations Agraires du Cayor à la Casamance*. St Yriex: Imprimérie Fabriqué.

Peil, M. 1974. Ghana's Aliens. *International Migration Review*. 8: 367–81.

Pollet, E. and Winter, G. 1971. *La Société Soninké (Dyahunu Mali)*. Brussells: Université Libre de Bruxelles.

Post, K. 1972. 'Peasantization' and Rural Political Movements in Western Africa, *Archives Européennes de Sociologie*, 13: 223–54.

Pottier, J. 1983. Defunct Labour Reserve? Mambwe Villages in the Post-Migration Economy, *Africa*, 53(2): 2–23.

Prioul, C. 1969. Les Cultures Maraichéres à Bangui, *Cahiers d'Outre-Mer*, 82: 191–202.

Rey, P. P. 1969. Articulation des Modes de Depéndence, et des Modes de Production dans Deux Sociétés Lignagères, *Cahiers d'Études Africaines*, 9: 415–40.

1975. The Lineage Mode of Production, *Critique of Anthropology*, 3, Spring.

Richards, A. L., Sturrock, F. and Fortt, J. M. (eds.), 1973. *Subsistence to Commercial Farming in Present Day Buganda: An Economic and Anthropological Survey*. Cambridge: Cambridge University Press.

Richards, P. 1983. Farming Systems and Agrarian Change in West Africa, *Progress in Human Geography*, 7(1), 1–39.

Roberts, R. and Klein, M. A. 1980. The Banamba Slave Exodus of 1906 and Decline of Slavery in the Western Sudan, *Journal of African History*, 21: 375–94.

Robertson, A. F. 1982. Abusa: The Structural History of an Economic Contract, *Journal of Development Studies*, 18(4): 447–78.

Rukandema, F. M. 1978. Resource Availability, Utilization and Productivity on Small-Scale Farms in Kakamega District, Western Kenya. Ph.D. thesis. Cornell University.

Sayer, A. 1983. Notes on Geography and the Relationship Between People and Nature. In *Society and Nature: Socialist Perspectives on the Relationship Between Human and Physical Geography*. London Group of the Union of Socialist Geographers.

Schildkraut, E. 1979. Women's Work and Children's Work: Variations Among Moslems in Kano. In S. Wallman (ed.), *Social Anthropology of Work*. London: Academic Press.

Seddon, D. (ed.) 1978. *Relations of Production: Marxist Approaches to Economic Anthropology*. London: Frank Cass.

Seibel, H. D. and Massing, A. 1974. *Traditional Organisations and Economic Development: Studies of Indigenous Co-operatives in Liberia*. New York: Praeger.

Shenton, R. W. and Lenihan, L. 1981. Capital and Class: Peasant Differentiation in Northern Nigeria, *Journal of Peasant Studies*, 9(1): 47–70.

Shepherd, A. 1981. Agrarian Change in Northern Ghana: Public Investment, Capitalist Farming and Famine. In J. Heyer, P. Roberts and G. Williams (eds.), *Rural Development in Tropical Africa.* New York: St Martin's Press.

Smith, M. G. 1955. *The Economy of the Hausa Communities of Zaria.* London: HMSO.

Smock, Audrey Chapman, 1981. Women's Economic Roles. In T. Killick, *Papers on the Kenyan Economy.* Nairobi: Heinemann.

Standing, G. (ed.). 1984. *Labour Circulation and the Labour Process.* London: Croom Helm.

Staudt, K. 1975. Women Farmers and Inequalities in Agricultural Services, *Rural Africana*, 29: 81–94.

Sumra, S. 1979. Problems of Agricultural Production in Handemi District. In K. S. Kim, T. B. Mabele and M. J. Schultheis (eds.), *Papers on the Political Economy of Tanzania.* Nairobi: Heinemann.

Suret-Canale, J. 1964. Les Sociétés Traditionelles en Afrique Tropicale et le Concept de Mode de Production Asiatique, *La Pensée*, 117: 21–42.

Sutherland, A. M. D. 1983. Personal Communication arising from fieldwork done in three villages in the periphery of Sokoto, Nigeria.

Swindell, K. 1978. Family Farms and Migrant Labour: The Strange Farmers of the Gambia, *Canadian Journal of African Studies*, 12(1), 3–17.

1980. Serawoollies, Tillibunkas and Strange Farmers. The Development of Migrant Groundnut Farming in the Gambia, *Journal of African History*, 21(1): 93–104.

1982. From Migrant Farmer to Permanent Settler: The Strange Farmers of The Gambia. In J. I. Clarke and L. A. Kosinski (eds.), *Redistribution of Population in Tropical Africa.* London: Heinemann.

1984. Dry season migration from north-west Nigeria, *Africa*, 54(1), 3–9.

Terray, E. 1972. *Marxism and Primitive Societies.* New York: Monthly Review Press.

Tiffen, M. 1976. *The Enterprising Peasant: Economic Development in Gombe Emirate.* London: HMSO.

Tosh, J. 1980. The Cash Crop Revolution in Tropical Africa: An Agricultural Re-appraisal, *African Affairs*, 79: 79–94.

Tourtre, R. 1954. Perfectionnement des Techniques Culturales au Senegal, *Annales du Centre de Recherches Agronomiques de Bambey au Senegal*, 13: 65.

Uchendu, V. C. 1970. Traditional Workgroups in Economic Development. Abstract of Paper Submitted to the University of East Africa Social Science Conference, Dar-es-Salaam.

Van Hear, N. 1982. Northern Labour and Development of Capitalist Agriculture in Ghana. Ph.D. thesis. University of Birmingham.

Vennetier, P. 1961. La Vie Agricole Urbaine à Pointe-Noire. *Cahiers d'Outre-Mer*, 14: 60–84.

Von Rotenhan, D. 1968. Cotton Farming in Sukumaland. In H. Ruthenberg (ed.), *Smallholder Farming and Smallholder Development in Tanzania*. Munich: Weltforum Verlag.

Wallace, T. 1979. Rural Development through Irrigation: Studies in a Town on the Kano River Project. Mimeo. Zaria, Nigeria: Centre for Social and Economic Research, Ahmadu Bello University.

1980. Agricultural Projects and Land in Northern Nigeria, *Revue of African Political Economy*, 17: 59–69.

Wallman, S. (ed.), 1979. *Social Anthropology of Work*. London: Academic Press.

Watts, S. 1980. Patterns of Rural – Rural Mobility in Central Kware State Nigeria. Unpublished MS, African Population Mobility Project, University of Liverpool.

Wedderburn, S. G. 1977. Personal Communication.

Weil, P. M. 1973. Wet Rice, Women and Adaptation in The Gambia, *Rural Africana*, (19): 20–9.

Williams, G. 1982. Taking the Part of Peasants. In J. Harris (ed.), *Rural Development: Theories of Peasant Economy and Agrarian Change*. London: Hutchinson.

Zachariah, K. C. and Condé, J. 1981. *Migration in West Africa: Demographic Aspects*. New York: Oxford University Press.

INDEX

The Politics of Africa's Economic Stagnation

RICHARD SANDBROOK

Director, Development Studies Programme, and Professor of Political Science at Scarborough College, University of Toronto

with JUDITH BARKER

African states are not, in any real sense, capitalist states. In post-colonial Africa one finds a form of neopatrimonialism – personal rule – that introduces a variety of economic irrationalities. This book analyses the social conditions impelling political adaptation and the consequences of personal rule for economic life, and surveys creative responses to the predicament African people now face.

The authors argue that personal rule is not simply a euphemism for ineptitude and mismanagement. They believe that it operates according to a particular rationality that shapes a ruler's actions when, in the absence of legitimate authority, he is confronted with the challenge of governing an unintegrated peasant society. Neopatrimonialism is essentially an adaptation of colonial-inspired political institutions to peculiar historical and social conditions, and this book focuses on the political factor as an important cause of Africa's economic ills.

Migrant Laborers

SHARON STICHTER
Associate Professor of Sociology, University of Massachusetts-Boston

This book surveys the literature on labour migration in east, west and southern Africa and interprets it from a political economy perspective. It addresses the controversies as to the origins of migrancy and its effects on the rural economy, emphasizing the differences in the response of various African precapitalist societies to wage labour, and the regional variations in the effects on the rural economy and on the division of labour within the rural household. Male migrants' experiences with forced labour, recruitment systems, advance payments, and compound controls are described, and the rather different character of women's migration is examined.

A central concern is the development of migrant workers' consciousness and forms of resistance. Labour protest among dockers, miners and domestic workers is examined and, finally, the persistence of migrancy in South Africa today is contrasted with the decline of labour migrancy in other parts of the continent.